D0803494

Idol Truth

Idol Truth

A MEMOIR

LEIF GARRETT

WITH CHRIS EPTING

Post Hill
PRESS

A POST HILL PRESS BOOK

Idol Truth:
A Memoir
© 2019 by Leif Garrett with Chris Epting
All Rights Reserved

ISBN: 978-1-64293-236-2
ISBN (eBook): 978-1-64293-237-9

Cover art by Cody Corcoran
Interior design and composition by Greg Johnson, Textbook Perfect
Interior photographs courtesy of the author.

Post Hill Press
New York • Nashville
posthillpress.com
Published in the United States of America

Contents

Introduction xi
Prologue 1

Part One: Before

Screams 5
Acting 9
Crash 12
My Three Sons 14
Bob & Carol & Ted & Alice 16
The First Real Break 18
Burt 21
Bed-Wetting 23
Per Diem 24
Escapes to the North 26
The Dating Game 28
Becoming a Busy Actor 30
Masturbation 32
School 34
Three for the Road 36
David MacLeod 38

Michael Lloyd: First Record 41

Israel 43

Losing My Virginity 46

Led Zeppelin 49

Shaun's Loss, My Gain 52

Peter Lundy 53

Back Up North: Moonlight 55

Part Two: During

The Scotti Brothers 59

Teen Magazines 62

Brad Elterman 66

Atlantic Records 68

The First Album 70

The First U.S. Promotional Tour 73

Magic Mountain 76

Sweet Sixteen 80

The First European Promotional Tour: London Hotel 82

Bad Habits 85

First Time in Japan: August 1978 89

Tenerife 92

John Belushi 96

Joe Perry 98

Skateboard 102

Australia 104

"Dead" Dad 109

The Attention 111

Charity 114

Feel the Need and "I Was Made for Dancing" 116

Family and *Wonder Woman* 118

Ali 120

Mysterious Illness 123

The First Concert 127

The Astrodome 130

Monique St. Pierre 133

Off the Wall. 135

The Leif Garrett Special 140

My Dinner with Brooke 144

Getting Out of Control. 148

The House 151

Car Burial 153

The Meeting 158

The 1979 Tour 163

"Dear Beautiful Boy" 169

Same Goes for You. 174

The Accident 176

Nicollette 182

Back on the Road: Japan and Europe 184

Korea 187

Queen 190

Rick Finch 193

The Photo 202

Nicollette Moves In 205

Brian Johnson 207

Long Shot 209

The Outsiders. 212

Money Talks 215

More John Belushi 216

Part Three: After

More Nicollette. 221

Roland Settlement 222

Shaker Run and Nicollette Breakup 223

The Road to Freedom: Scientology 227

Justine Bateman 231

Jason Bateman Road Trip 234

Heroin. 236

Night with Robert Downey Jr. 238

Elaine 242

Working in a Bike Shop 245

Intervention 247

Reunion? 251

1997: Dave Navarro, Billy Zane, Marilyn Manson 253

1997: Chris Farley 255

1998: The Death of David MacLeod 258

Behind the Music 260

What You Do for Money 266

Arrests 268

2010: Back to Korea 273

Epilogue 275

Postscript 277

Afterword by Chris Epting 281

"Every experience is a lesson.
Every loss is a gain."

—SATHYA SAI BABA

"And when they played they really played.
And when they worked they really worked."

—DR. SEUSS

Introduction

My bedroom is womblike: all dark wood and sealed off on the bottom floor of the house, overflowing with my stuff. A box of 1970s concert T-shirts with my picture on them. Old stage costumes. Lots of CDs and obscene amounts of Hot Wheels and old backstage passes and all-access laminates. I recently took lots of things out of storage and it surrounds me, mingled with newer purchases like candle holders, incense, and other Zen-like items. My personal cave. I live high up in the wild canyons of Los Angeles, with Malibu below on one side and the San Fernando Valley below on the other. At the top of this mountain, my rustic house feels like an aerie. Being nestled up in the trees like this has always made me feel safe and secure. My clock blinks 2:07 a.m. As usual, I'm restless and having a hard time sleeping. Maybe it's the generations of ghosts from my past that find some perverse pleasure in both haunting and taunting me. Whatever it may be, it's the dead of night and I'm wide awake, edgy, and alone in my bed.

A full moon in a deep blue summer sky bathes the ancient woods outside in a silvery light. The young bushy-tailed coyote on my property that has accepted me as a friend is yipping somewhere on the hill. Beyond that, all is quiet and still. My orange-brown cat, a formerly feral warrior named Gizmo, aka "Walter Kitty," pads over to me before settling in at the end of the bed—like me, restless and instinctively on guard. Then I get a strange urge. I pick up the iPad a friend gave me. I've sort of sworn off technology, holding out for the longest time in even getting a cell phone because I just did not want to be bothered. I like working with my hands. Painting, writing—crafting things. I always have. Computers have always left me cold. Still, there's this strange urge. I power up the slim machine and the screen illuminates my face, pale blue light in the dark, tightening my pupils. I'm curious.

I click a link and then all of a sudden there I am. The child actor. I've never done this before. I've never sat and clicked on myself. On the right of the screen other clips of me sit there, waiting for me to choose them. So I do, one after another. There I am in so many movies and TV shows in the 1970s. *The Odd Couple. The Dating Game.* There I am on *The Waltons.* I keep clicking. Other people have home movies; I have Hollywood productions to chart my growth, along with European and Asian productions—basically things from everywhere except the Arctic. My parents and siblings change from scene to scene. A handful of additional clicks and the shy, sensitive young actor magically transforms into the late-1970s teen idol/sex symbol. I have never done this before. And it's making me anxious. Nervous even. There I am chatting with Dick Clark on *American Bandstand.* Seamlessly, I dissolve from being in Japan to being in Australia, then Germany, Korea, England, prancing and sashaying across stages while singing my big top-ten hit, "I Was Made for Dancing." Then I come across a video graphic: "Leif." It's my network TV special when I was just eighteen years old, with Bob Hope. There I am at the London Palladium doing a comedy bit with the master. I was the youngest person ever at that time to have his own network special. Girls are screaming for me. There I am doing comedy with Brooke Shields and Marie Osmond. Another click and there I am with Tatum O'Neal. Models. Playmates. Old girlfriends and lovers. Nicollette Sheridan. I found something beautiful in all of them, and I wanted them all.

I keep clicking. Like so often in my life, I get addicted. I see myself growing older. It hits me: My life is literally flashing before my eyes.

And then I get to those clips. The ones that I never wanted to see. The ones in which I have become addicted to heroin. I'm watching myself as a man now, and I'm watching myself lying to people in a series of interviews. There's a news clip about my arrest. That damned mug shot. Then I get to the documentary, the one it seemed like the whole world watched about me. The big one. I'm sitting there on camera saying that I was clean. But I wasn't. I just wish that I wasn't the only one that thought no one else knew. I was kidding myself and it wasn't funny. That was my secret; at least I thought it was. Did everyone know? Was I kidding myself? The night that show first aired, back in 1999, Jane's Addiction guitarist Dave Navarro had a viewing party at his infamous Hollywood Hills house, where we had been doing drugs for years. I had to leave the room. I couldn't stand to watch myself betraying myself. (And Dave, I'm sorry about nabbing that ball of tar heroin you left out for someone to steal. I fell for it hook, line, and sinker; you know how addicts are always jonesing with no money in their pockets).

Alone in the dark, it's becoming more and more obvious just how many truths I have kept in over the years. Not just from those around me, but most important, from myself. I've denied and buried so much. Decades' worth of emotions, stories, deceit; layers of joy and pain.

Behind those flickering images, I now see a story in front of me, and I know it's finally time to tell that story. There's no more time to waste. No more running from the past. There are no more people to be scared of. No more abusers to hide from. I'm tired of the ghosts. I'm ready to confront everyone and everything. I'm also ready to relive the magic that I got to experience, and there was a lot of it. I decide in that moment that these ghosts need to come out. All of them. So they will.

Prologue

The sickening screams were coming at me in stereo. About fifty feet down the hill, my friend Roland's voice, though muffled inside my flipped-over black Porsche 911, still managed to pierce the cool November air. "Get me out of here," he wailed. "I can't feel my legs."

Up near the top of the hill, where I had just managed to climb in search of an emergency call box, the family whose car we had clipped just before rolling down the embankment was standing outside their car. The father was yelling at me, "What the hell were you doing? You could have killed us." Down below, Roland's screams kept wafting up, fainter but still there. The screams of anger and screams of agony transformed a normal night into a nightmare. Just an hour earlier, I had been on top of the world. I was the one everyone desired. I was a jet-set pop star, a pinup, a platinum-haired teen idol with gold and platinum records to back it all up. In this moment right after the crash, scarred and scared, I felt everything being stripped away and my truth being revealed. The singing career, the teen idol—it was all a fraud, a fantasy concocted by adults who knew how to make money but knew nothing about protecting a child. I wasn't that made-up androgynous fantasy on countless *Tiger Beat* magazine covers. I wasn't even a singer. I was an actor, and a good one. I was also, at that moment, a petrified, confused, lonely seventeen-year-old kid on a hillside in the middle of a horrifying Hollywood night that was getting worse by the second. I was also a functioning alcoholic and a drug addict, already hooked on Quaaludes, pot, and cocaine. I had everything, but I had nothing. The screams continued, rattling both sides of my brain, tearing at the seams of my dwindling sanity. I never could stand the sound of screams.

Part One

BEFORE

Screams

The sound of screams had me shaking as I hid under the table in our tiny kitchen; my dad's raging abuse of my beautiful mom is one of the first things I can remember hearing as a young child. "Your life belongs to me, so don't ever think about leaving with my kids. Because if you do, I'll hunt you down with a bottle of acid and throw it right in your pretty little face." Blaring, hurtful words designed to inflict pain and fear, relentlessly torturing my mom and terrifying both me and my younger sister, Dawn. We were used to screams, but that didn't make being in this horrific environment any easier.

I came into the world on November 8, 1961, a loud and feisty Scorpio born smack in the middle of Hollywood. It was my mom, Carolyn, who gave me my name because it means "beloved" in Norse. My middle name, Per, means "rock," also "strength." As my mom tells it, I did everything early. At six months I was swimming in the pool, at ten months I was walking, and at a year and a half I was speaking in complete sentences. No time to waste. I'm the same way today.

My sister, Dawn, was born fourteen months later. Most of the memories I have of my dad, Rick, involve yelling at and berating my mother. Automatically, I was protective of her. Maybe it's because she's a fellow Scorpio, or maybe it's simply the special bond that I think exists between most mothers and sons. Fathers seem to decide, early on, what they want their sons to be, in many cases. Mothers, I would suggest, are more given to allowing their sons to bloom into what they naturally are destined to be.

Regardless, it was hellish at home.

I remember a trip to the Grand Canyon when Dawn, just a couple of years old, dropped something over the rail. My father held her by her ankles upside down, taunting and tormenting her, even shaming her for daring to make a simple mistake. Even in my young mind, I wanted to be away from this situation.

Thankfully, when I was five years old, my mother packed us up and we left him. Or he left us. It's hard to be sure what happened, but my family did become separated at that point. The lack of a father figure is something I have struggled with my entire life, and looking back, I am sorry things started out this way in my life. But there was no other choice. My mother had to survive, and she wanted to protect us from what was going on. I know it was hard for her. She came from a generation in which many women were scared to speak out against men. Her upbringing reinforced much of that attitude. Women were subservient to men and oftentimes, like children, they were to be seen and not heard. Leaving my father was a very big deal for her, and I think it took a lot of guts. Being a single mother with two children in the mid-1960s was a far more radical decision than it is today.

My mom was a costume designer by trade, so the next couple of years for us were spent in an artistic, almost bohemian kind of existence. We had very little money (my dad was not providing support), so we lived in an eighty-dollar-a-month house in what was called a shack flats community, lots of small old bungalows, near Hollywood. There was a diverse cast of characters surrounding us: two female impersonators, a bongo drummer, singers, actresses, and a musical group called the Mushrooms, who would later go on to become Seals and Crofts. It was a highly theatrical and dramatic environment, and even at that young age, I related to them. I liked the crazy, open, free-thinking spirit that they all seemed to embrace.

I also liked the fact that my mom was so artistic. She grew up near San Francisco and originally made clothes for herself and even Dawn and me. But soon, in Hollywood, she found herself designing outfits for Marlo Thomas, Judy Carne, Burt Reynolds, and many other actors and performers. The more she worked, the easier it became for us to move into a slightly nicer apartment. We moved a bunch of times during this period, but we really settled in when she found a $125-a-month house in a fairly nice family neighborhood in Burbank.

I was a handful back then, and I know it. I fell in love with skate-boarding, and I was constantly getting scraped and scratched up. I had plenty of accidents that required stitches, and I broke my nose more than once. I was basically a sports freak and one of those kids who actually picked things up pretty quickly. Whether it was baseball or football or skateboarding, I seemed to be a natural athlete. And every-body would tell me that! I also loved playing with my Hot Wheels, and cars in general held a basic fascination for me. I had an early love for speed, thrills, and spills, with no fear of any of them. I was rambunc-tious and even a little reckless. I would jump from windows in our apartment into the swimming pool—and not just from our apartment. I would visit neighbors and do the same thing from their windows too. I was a daredevil, and even though I was basically shy and quiet on the outside, on the inside I was a bit of a wild child.

I didn't like conforming to what everybody wanted me to be. By the age of six I had started wearing my hair a little bit long, and at school some of the kids—and even some of the parents—would give me a hard time because they thought I looked like a girl. I was an average student, but I wasn't crazy about school. I liked thinking about all of the creative people we had grown up around; their lives seemed to have far fewer barriers and rules. That appealed to me.

My favorite memories around this time were going up north to the San Francisco area to be with my mom's family. That's where I really got to be a kid—where I would hang out with my cousins and their friends. They lived by the bay in Marin County, and my uncle co-owned Edgewater Yacht Sales, which meant we were on the water

Doing a kick turn on a small ramp with my 3ft Sims downhill board with Gullwing trucks, in bellbottoms.

a lot. It was so much fun to hang out with all the kids up there, especially my cousin, Peter. He was my hero from day one. He's about five years older than me, and I always knew he was special. He was a true alpha male: incredibly good-looking, very athletic, and truly charismatic. In the absence of any real male influence in my life, I looked up to Peter from the moment I met him. Everybody up there called him "Peter Perfect." Peter had such an effect on me.

Acting

My mom and sister and I settled into our new life together. We didn't talk to my father, and we never heard from him. In a way, it was like he no longer existed. I guess that was the best way to have it back then, but looking back, I can't stress how different I wish things had been. As important as a relationship is with your mother, little boys also need their dads. They need somebody to teach them how to be a man. Little girls also need their dads, and I know that my sister, even though she shares the harsh memories that we grew up with, inside really wished things had been different too. As a result of the three of us living together, I became fiercely protective of both my mom and my sister.

My mom would occasionally date guys, but nothing ever got too serious. My mom was focused on providing for us, and even though she worked primarily behind the scenes as a costumer, given her physical beauty, it's no surprise that eventually she was asked to step in front of the camera and try acting. This became a pivotal moment not just for her but for Dawn and me as well. See, her agent at that time, after learning my mom had two cute kids at home, suggested we all get headshots and take a stab at this acting thing. Hey, it sounded like fun to me. If it worked out, it would get me out of school and put me back around a bunch of creative and crazy people, similar to what I remembered so fondly from my earliest years. So when she asked me, "Would you like to do this?" I was all in. As was Dawn.

In 1966, I did my first commercial at age five for Metropolitan Life. It was awesome. It was filmed on a merry-go-round in Griffith Park, near where we lived. That led to some other commercials, including for Continental Airlines, Mattel, and even a Sears commercial with Dawn. My sister also began landing parts and commercials, and soon the two of us were constantly being driven all around town, being sent to auditions by our agent. It was fun. Both of us had no problem memorizing lines, and we actually enjoyed the process. I wasn't one of those kids who was a born performer or anything. Obviously, my mom was encouraging us to do this, and so that made it seem like a good idea. Is it what I wanted to be when I was kid? Absolutely not. I wanted to be an athlete. Maybe a skier or football player. I loved sports that much. But acting was cool, and on the sets of the commercials I would get to talk to guys who were building things and doing all of the technical and construction work, which to me was interesting. In a way, those workers on the sets, just like it would be later on when I started doing movies, were good male role models for me. They would patiently answer my questions, which were many, and did what they could to make me feel comfortable.

And so we spent a lot of our time going from casting call to casting call in the hopes of getting more work. The teachers at my school, Carpenter Elementary, hated the fact that we were constantly being pulled out for work, but that's just how it was. School presented other issues as well. The guys there were always making trouble for me, taunting me because I was an actor and also because girls seemed to gravitate toward me. That's right, even before I became a teen idol, girls were drawn to me, and I loved that. Even as a kid I would daydream about being with girls, and around this time I actually had my first sexual dream/fantasy. It involved a crush I had, on Jennifer, whom I envisioned emerging out of a steamy mist before falling into my arms. But the fact that girls liked me did create hassles for me. I learned early on how to use humor to deflect and sidestep the jealous scorn I'd get from other guys. It would come in handy years later.

I did have a good friend at school though, Rhett Winchell, the son of the founder of Winchell's Donuts. He and I both loved cars and would spend hours drawing pictures of hot rods and talking about our priceless collections of Hot Wheels, the popular die-cast toy racing cars. But when I wasn't dodging bullies, thinking about girls, or drawing cars with Rhett, I would be back in the car with my mom. We would drive around all day from audition to audition to callback to callback. The car radio was always on, and I remember the very first song that made me sit up and take notice. It was "Cherry Hill Park" by Billy Joe Royal. Something about that song got to me. I was about seven years old, and the very first time I heard it, I loved it. It wasn't that big a hit, but it did get played every so often. This song is about a girl named Mary Hill who has a bunch of sexual liaisons with boys at a place called Cherry Hill Park (inspired by a real place, Cherry Hill, New Jersey). To this day when I hear that song, it takes me back. A switch flipped that day for me in the car. All of a sudden, music mattered to me. Even though I was an actor and that's how most of my time was spent, the sly, suggestive lyrics and slinky melody sucked me right in. Whatever I would end up doing in life, the music I would listen to would help shape and sculpt every emotion I had; that much I knew. Soon, it would be Led Zeppelin and Elton John, but thanks to Billy Joe Royal, my eyes, ears, and musical heart had been opened.

Crash

My career almost ended before it even started. Hell, my life nearly ended with it too. It was October 2, 1968. I was six years old. My mom and sister and I were visiting Twentieth Century Fox in Los Angeles. Dawn was there reading for a part in a new television series, *Nanny and the Professor*. I went inside with them and up to the casting offices on the second floor of the two-story building. Out the window, I spied what looked like some monkey bars out in front of the building (they were actually just metal bars that were part of the building's entry structure), and so I asked my mom if I could go out and play on them. I didn't feel like being cooped up inside waiting with them. It wasn't like today; you could actually do stuff like that and it was pretty safe. Plus, it was on the lot, so it was a fairly secure environment. My mom said fine, so I raced back outside.

Outside in the warm sun, I was climbing and swinging around when all of a sudden, I saw a small airplane approaching that appeared to be flying closer to the ground than it should have been. It was such a strange sight. Even though it was a single-engine plane, it was flying low enough that, as it approached, I could actually see the pilot. And something was wrong. He had a pained look on his face. He was clutching his chest, and then he fell over onto the console in front of him. I literally saw him go unconscious as the plane passed not thirty feet over my head before crashing right into the second floor of the administration building. Right near the office where my mom and sister had been. There was a huge orange explosion as it collided with the building, then fiery debris, glowing and sinister, began raining down from the sky. It was terrifying. Small pieces of burning metal kept finding my clothes, stinging my skin. I could smell the acrid odor of burning hair and realized that some of my hair was burning. And of course absolute chaos broke out all around me. The plane had just missed crashing into the lavish street set for the movie *Hello, Dolly!*, which was packed with production workers and actors at the time of the crash. As scared as I was, feeling the red-hot bits of debris on my skin, I was most scared for my mom and sister. Had they been killed? I didn't know what to do. All of the adults rushing around me paid no attention to me.

I was crying and yelling for my mom and sister, wailing in the madness. In the chaos, I saw my mom come running out of the building looking desperately for me. To this day I'm not sure I've ever been so happy in my life. She grabbed me and hugged me and kissed me. She told me that at the last minute, they had moved to a room on the other side of the building, thus sparing them. With my sister in tow, we rushed off the lot.

This day that could have been so tragic for all of us actually wound up playing a big part in what happened next with my family. Dawn would get that role in *Nanny and the Professor*, playing Prudence Everett. She escaped with a job. I got away with my life.

My Three Sons

In 1969, when the television pilot for *Nanny and the Professor* did not initially sell, Dawn was released from her contract with ABC. She was then cast as Dodie Douglas in the long-running family comedy television series *My Three Sons*. ABC sued unsuccessfully to get her to perform in *Nanny and the Professor* after she had already been cast for *My Three Sons*. *My Three Sons* had been on the air since 1960, and in a foretelling of how many other TV series over the years would try to inject some life into a show that was approaching the end, they introduced a cute new character. Remember when *The Partridge Family* introduced Ricky Stevens? Or when *The Brady Bunch* introduced cousin Oliver? This was before all of that, and it made Dawn famous almost instantly. I was very proud of her, but I was also a little bit jealous. She was younger than I was, we had both been going to a lot of screen tests and auditions, and just like that, she was part of a hit TV series. That's what I wanted. But we all benefited from it. I would get to go to the set and watch her work, and there was also some travel involved that I got to take part in as well. I remember a fun trip to Phoenix for a charity event all of the actors were taking part in. My mom obviously liked it because it provided a steady income for us, and that helped us through what were becoming some fairly lean years.

One thing that happened to Dawn on *My Three Sons* provided another glimpse into the future: how they marketed the doll that she played with on the show. Remember Myrtle? Well, Myrtle was actually marketed by Mattel and was one of the most popular toys of the year. But there was an issue: Dawn's image was included on the packaging, but she never received any money for that. My mother (and I suppose our agent as well) was not savvy about things like licensing and merchandising, so she missed out on that opportunity. It was that kind of lack of awareness that would ultimately cause me problems as well, but that was still a few years away.

Bob & Carol & Ted & Alice

The very first time I ever found myself in front of a movie camera was in the fall of 1968, shooting what would become a very important cultural cinematic moment, *Bob & Carol & Ted & Alice*. My mom wasn't able to be on set with me this time because she actually had landed her own part in a movie called *The Love God?* starring Don Knotts at Universal. Dawn was busy working on that pilot for *Nanny and the Professor*. It was a busy time for all of us, but I was excited to have gotten the part, even though if you blink while watching the film today, you just might miss me. Being around all of those great actors, Elliott Gould and Robert Culp—and especially Dyan Cannon and Natalie Wood—was exciting for me.

The film was directed by Paul Mazursky and would eventually go on to earn four Academy Award nominations in 1970. The music was done by Quincy Jones, and the film was a big deal all the way around. I developed a serious schoolboy crush on Dyan Cannon, who was very sweet with me. She gave me an autographed photo that I still have today. Natalie Wood was also lovely and absolutely beautiful. Even at the young age of seven, I remember appreciating the sultry beauty of these women. I know that sounds strange, but I've always been comfortable around women and have always been attracted to them—especially older women, but more on that later. The film was a breakthrough for how it dealt with the touchy subject of open marriage and sexual experimentation. It was truly ahead of its time, and for me it was a great chance to watch Hollywood at its highest level, up close and personal. Even though my part was tiny, I was there, I was observing, and it made me want to be a successful actor. I wanted to grow up and do what these people around me were doing.

The First Real Break

My first real break on television came in December 1968, when I was cast in a pilot called *Anderson and Company*. I almost missed out. The boy who was originally cast was only five years old, and due to labor laws in California, he couldn't work as many hours as a six-year-old, which is what I was. His loss was my gain. It was directed by Gene Reynolds of *M*A*S*H* fame. The show wasn't picked up, which made me kind of sad, but it felt good to get the good notices I received from the production team. They thought I had some talent. I also learned then that getting used to rejection was part of the deal.

My next television gig was on *Medical Center* starring Chad Everett. My mom in the episode was Dyan Cannon, whom I had appeared with in *Bob & Carol & Ted & Alice*. It was great seeing her again; that was the good part. The bad part was that the second assistant director played a joke on me that wound up costing me TV work for at least a couple of years. He said to me at one point, "Look, Leif, you need to do this scene naked." I didn't know what he was talking about. In the scene, I was to be wearing a hospital gown, and he was telling me I couldn't have anything on underneath. This scared me. I couldn't stand the thought of being naked under there with all of these people around me. Strangers. Adults. I was shy and modest. So I broke down crying. He said he was only joking, but it upset me. I think it was a truly stupid thing to do to a kid. I must have melted down because it cost me the job. Once it got around that I was "difficult," it cost me. Even now I think that was a stupid joke for that guy to play.

Something else that was working against me at that time was another actor named Johnny Whitaker, the redhead with all those freckles who was in the TV show *Family Affair*, in addition to many other shows and movies (I was in an episode of *Family Affair* with him). He was the most popular "type" of the day. I didn't look like that all. I didn't have that folksy, Huck Finn kind of appearance. I had long blond hair, and a lot of people thought I was a girl. That worked against me. I think I screen-tested at Disney six times and never got anything because I didn't look like a country bumpkin.

One thing I got used to almost immediately was the idea of rejection and failure, especially when my sister was getting cast in things left and right in addition to starring in *My Three Sons*. She was hot, and I was not. That said, I kept at it, at one point doing ten screen tests in a row without getting one of the jobs. The most memorable of those failures was in 1969, when I tested with Lucille Ball for the film *Mame*. The casting director liked my acting, but because I couldn't sing, didn't cast me in the film. That one was disappointing. At Disney, I read for everything: *Bayou Boy, Pomeroy's People, The Burtons Abroad, Escape to Witch Mountain*, and several more without getting cast. It was always something: I was too pretty. I wasn't rugged enough. I looked like a girl.

But then things started to click. In 1970 I earned a bit part in a movie called *Takers*, and my mom was hired as the clothing designer. Then I was in a film called *The Counselor*. The more sets I was on, the more I enjoyed the work. On set, it was always fun to hang out with the carpenters and electricians and all the other workers who would show me things like how to hammer a nail or how to paint. I loved that. They taught me little things that boys were supposed to know how to do. Thinking back on it today, a lot of those workers became like surrogate fathers to me.

Our home life obviously became a blur. Dawn was working constantly, I was getting busier with my own gigs, and my mom had costuming jobs as well. Our household was kind of like a TV series all its own. I landed a leading role in the first *Walking Tall* film in 1972, which was going to be shot in Tennessee. Dawn was cast as well, I think because the producers realized that by hiring both of us, they would save money because my mom would be the only chaperone needed for two actors. I loved working with Dawn. We got along great, and it was easier because we could go over dialogue at home, which helped a lot. It gave us an edge. My mom taught us a great actor's trick: She'd have us read our lines as the last thing we did before sleep. We'd walk on the next day and the lines would be memorized. We wound up doing all three *Walking Tall* films together, and those were fantastic. In 1973, Max Baer (he was Jethro on *The Beverly Hillbillies*) was producing and starring in a film called *Macon County Line*. What really bothered me in that film was that I had to have a 1950s military haircut. I tried to convince Max that a wig would take care of it, but Max said no way. So off I went to have my hair sheared at CBS studios. It killed me to look in the mirror and watch the butchering. I actually did wear a wig for a while when I went back to school; I was that embarrassed.

Burt

In the early 1970s, my mom started dating Burt Reynolds. She had known him on and off during the 1960s, but when their relationship started, she fell completely and totally in love with him. At one point she traveled east to visit him on the set of a film he was making called *Deliverance*, in South Carolina. Of all the people she dated while I was growing up (not that there were that many), Burt was the one who stood out to me because he was around the most, he was the most consistent, and he seemed concerned with trying to make all of our lives better. He would recommend agents and managers and financial advisors, and he would take time to play with us and make us feel loved. At Christmastime, I remember, he gave both Dawn and me a big box each. We eagerly opened our boxes, and there was another box inside. Inside that, another box. It was like a Russian nesting doll. We kept opening box after box after box until finally, we opened the smallest box and found fifty crisp one-dollar bills. We were thrilled. That was Burt. He had a fun sense about life and was good with kids. I liked him a lot because he seemed like a "real man." He was into sports, and he seemed like somebody I could aspire to be like. When their relationship ended around 1973, my mom was heartbroken. In fact, I had never seen her so upset. I understand what she saw in Burt.

Dawn, Burt, Mom, and me. What do I have, dyslexia? Or is my heart on the other side?

He was confident and he was successful. Seeing her get as upset as she did upset me as well. My relationship with my mom has always been very complicated, and growing up without a father figure, I was confused about my role in the household, especially when I became—for all intents and purposes—the man of the house. Even if I didn't know my place in the family structure, my mom, a Scorpio just like me, loved her children as much as a mother could, and we were a very close family. That's why watching her go through this breakup was so hard. This was somebody she wanted to be with, but she couldn't have him. In a way, though, I was okay with that. Because honestly, I didn't want anybody taking my mom away from me.

Bed-Wetting

Something I have never shared with anyone is that when I was six or seven years old, I became a bed-wetter. Looking back, I'm sure it had to do with a lot of the emotional trauma I had been through. The breakup of my family was a huge deal to me. It was a shattering experience, and it's only now that I can look back and understand the damage that it probably caused. And then you have the plane crash incident. And the rejections I'd receive after auditions. Reading about this condition today, I'm quite sure that all of these factors led to the fact that I wet my bed on a fairly regular basis throughout a large part of my childhood. My mom would talk to me about it, try to explain to me that when I got the urge, I needed to get up and go to the bathroom. But it didn't work. I couldn't control it. I was a deep sleeper then, and it would just happen, and I wasn't sure if it would ever be controlled. That is, until I was about twelve. At that point, my mom purchased a strange device, essentially an electric blanket that would create a shock against my body whenever I would wet the bed. And we're not talking a little shock either. This was a pretty serious jolt, as I remember. But you know what? It worked. After several weeks with this strange contraption, my bed-wetting ended.

Per Diem

I'll never forget the first time it happened. On my very first film set, I was handed an envelope at one point during a break in the shooting. "Here's your per diem, Leif." If you don't know, a per diem is an allotment of cash given to actors by the producers on the days when they are working. Back then it would vary from twenty to forty to sometimes as much as a hundred dollars a day. The point of a per diem is so that you have money to buy lunch or some other meal or anything else you might need while you're working. It's basically an allowance to cover living expenses. But even when I was a kid, what always struck me as funny was that when you're working on a film location, everything is taken care of. The catering tables feature some of the best food and snacks you will ever experience; there is nothing you are left wanting for. And yet, every day you get that envelope. "Here's your per diem, Leif." I think this was my favorite part of being an actor. I would look at that envelope and think about what I wanted to spend it on. Maybe I would save up for a new bicycle. Maybe there was a new album out that I wanted. The money I was making as an actor was supposed to have been automatically put into a trust fund, but since my mom got no child support, we used a lot of the money to help at home. But not the per diem. That was basically mine.

At about twelve years old, I wanted nothing more than a decent stereo. I wanted to experience albums like *Goodbye Yellow Brick Road* and *Led Zeppelin II* on a decent stereo system, or hi-fi, as stereos were called back then. I got lost in those albums, staring at the inner-sleeve artwork and devouring liner notes. One night, I snuck out of our apartment and walked several blocks to a local stereo shop. Using some per diem money, I secretly bought a stereo and snuck it back to the apartment. It's so funny; I was bringing it in like contraband, as if my mother wasn't going to know about it once I started cranking one of my albums. A neighbor of ours, a cool guy maybe in his early twenties who had turned me on to the band Humble Pie, saw me sneaking in with the box and said I looked like a thief. After I snuck it in, I got the stereo set up in my room and put on *Goodbye Yellow Brick Road*. As the first strains of "Funeral for a Friend" started to waft out of the speakers, I lay back on my bed and got lost in the music. My mom was seriously mad at me once she discovered what I had done. She thought I had sold off some of my possessions to obtain it. She didn't stop to think I had been pocketing per diem money. As I got older and the per diems got bigger, I would eventually buy things like a new bicycle, clothes that I wanted, and other luxury items that made me feel good.

But nothing was ever as cool as that stereo I bought with that special money that came in the envelope.

Escapes to the North

I loved going on location and going to the studios. I loved seeing people in different costumes and watching people build sets. Everything looked interesting and fun; it was way better than being cooped up in the classroom. It's amazing how much I learned making movies and television shows like *Family Affair*, *Cannon*, and many others. I met all kinds of interesting people, and it was never boring. Being an actor was always exciting and interesting. Working on sets was basically my first real memories in life. But nothing was as much fun as going up to the Bay Area to visit my family. I always loved going up to Northern California to visit my cousins Peter, Jim, Steven, Denise, Michael, Mark, and the rest of my family. Life down in Los Angeles was fun, but it was also a lot of work. There was a lot of running around, auditions, callbacks, meetings—it was almost like being an adult. Up north, it was totally different. Up there, I was just one of the gang. Nobody treated me any differently, and I was allowed to be myself. That was the thing about acting: I was always busy being someone else. But Peter never treated me any differently because I was on television or in movies. I would go up there and everybody was thrilled to see me, and we would get back on our boats and ride our bikes and do all of the great things that made me feel like a kid. Acting was something I liked, but it did feel a bit like I was being robbed of my childhood to some degree. I was always around adults and I was always busy studying my lines. I enjoyed it, but I also liked the opportunity to just be a kid, and up north, it was all about being a kid. We'd work on the boats (mostly old Chris-Crafts), caulking and sanding all day long. One summer my uncle Ken rented an amazing houseboat that we lived in on the Sacramento delta. Other times we'd all be out racing in our little Spitfire boats. Peter had his own flat-bottom ski boat that he would take me out in to teach me how to water-ski; it was awesome.

I do remember one time up there, though, that shocked me to my core and challenged all of the sweet innocence that I had been experiencing with my "gang." I must've been about eleven years old and as we were all hanging out, I watched as Peter accepted a joint from one of the other kids who was part of our group. I got so upset: tears in my eyes and everything. My mother had always told me that drugs were bad and I should never do them. That was drilled into me at a young age. And now here was my hero, the big brother I never had, hitting a joint in front of me. Why would he do this? What if my mother found out? It was confusing for me. On the one hand I wanted to be like Peter, but his behavior went against everything I'd been taught. I started thinking, *If Peter is doing it, maybe it's okay.* Once I got over the initial shock, it didn't seem that bad. Peter was everything to me. I remember afterward, on the way home, he knew I was upset. "It's okay, Leif," he said, cool as ever. "It's not a big deal. It's not going to lead to anything else, and it's not going to make me crazy. A lot of kids do it, and it's okay." He made me feel a little bit better. And now I wanted to try it.

The Dating Game

When I was nine years old, I was invited to appear on the popular TV show *The Dating Game*. My mom didn't think anything of it. This show was popular, and it was obviously a good chance at some national exposure. It was a special Halloween episode in 1971 that also featured the actor Vincent Price as the other guy who would get to choose from a selection of three bachelorettes. What I remember about that experience is not good at all. I was dressed up in an American Indian costume, and my three potential dates were also in costumes. This is one of those things that I look back on and say, "How could this have even happened?" How on earth were nine-year-olds being put in situations in which one of them was going to be chosen for a special date? Why were they sending children out on dates in the first place? Even worse were the questions they had written for me to ask each of the girls. The questions were loaded with double entendres and suggestive language. The show host, Jim Lange, was leering over me, practically drooling as he waited for me to ask questions and then ultimately choose the girl I would take on a date. At one point, he said to me lasciviously, "Boy, I bet she looks great in a bikini, huh, Leif?" I'm serious. It's easy to look up the video. I wish my mother had said no to this gig, but more than that, I wish the whole thing never existed in the first place. No kid deserves this kind of nonsense.

For the record, I messed up and actually meant to choose bachelorette number two. I just got confused. The girl who won the date with me brought a friend with her that day, and we spent it at Disneyland, courtesy of the show. Of course, it wasn't a date. I brought a friend with me too, and the boys did what they wanted and the girls did what they wanted. We were nine years old! That's actually the only normal part of the story, that we didn't actually go on a date.

The early '70s is a wonderful era that, for the most part, I recall quite fondly. The music was amazing. Great television shows and pretty good movies were being produced too. But our country had an attitude back then that allowed for this sort of thing. The people in charge didn't stop to think for a minute that maybe this messed with our minds a little bit. Being a kid and starting to develop crushes was already awkward enough. We didn't need to be seen by millions of people asking questions written by adults—questions that, in my mind, were designed to titillate the audience. There are a lot of things I wish I hadn't done back then. *The Dating Game* is right at the top of the list. It pains me to watch this today. It literally makes me sick to my stomach. I watch myself try to hop up into that chair, not even sure why I was there. I listen to the reactions of the crowd in response to the suggestive questions and answers, and I feel like my head's going to explode. What were the writers thinking when they put together those questions? Why was it okay to use children in this way back then?

Becoming a Busy Actor

About two years after that fiasco with *Medical Center*, I started getting a lot of TV parts. I was on many shows, including *Arnie*, *FBI*, *Cannon*, *Gunsmoke*, *The Smith Family*, *Apple's Way*, *Run, Joe, Run*, and many more. Looking back on those days, it seems pretty amazing that I worked with the likes of everyone from Henry Fonda to James Arness to the wonderful Tony Randall on the show *The Odd Couple*, on which I played his son, Leonard. Of all the actors I worked with back then, Tony took a real interest in me and my acting craft. I was so scared because I was used to doing either films or TV shows where there was no audience. *The Odd Couple* was shot live in front of a studio audience, and that scared me. I had never performed in front of people before, but Tony took me aside and explained to me how to wait for the applause to die down; he taught me things about timing, and he was very complimentary about my little ad-libs. Looking back, of all of the actors I've worked with, I have to say that Tony Randall is one of the most generous, most thoughtful people I have ever shared a screen with. Again, for a little boy who was always desperately looking for a father figure, I don't think he even knew how his actions affected me. I was so hungry for male attention that when someone like Tony Randall went out of his way to help teach me and guide me, well, I don't think he ever had any idea what he did for me.

I also enjoyed working with Martin Sheen on the set of the 1975 film *The Last Survivors*. What was fun about that shoot is that it was done at Paramount Studios in the giant lake on the soundstage. This was a unique production to be involved with. We would spend long periods in the water. Everybody would get pruned pretty good, shriveled up all over while being cold all the time. I don't think the adults were as crazy about it, but for me it was like a total adventure. They had a big wave machine going, and machines that made artificial thunder and lightning; it was a cool experience. Martin Sheen was one of the nicest guys I ever worked with. He was always joking around with me and made sure I was comfortable. He'd see "LG" on my robe and call me Little Guy.

Masturbation

I have to admit, once I started masturbating at around the age of eleven, I pretty much became obsessed with it. Anytime I was on a set where there were pretty older women, it got my heart racing. And I would take those feelings home. I didn't have a lock on my door, so I had to be careful. I also didn't have much access to any kind of stimulating reading material, if you know what I mean. My mom subscribed to *Cosmopolitan* magazine, and if I recall correctly, on page three of each issue, there was always an image of a voluptuous woman. That's what did it for me. I also managed to get my hands on a copy of *Playboy* magazine when I was around twelve. I'm kind of ashamed to admit it today because of how strongly I feel about people taking things that aren't theirs, but yes, I swiped the magazine from a local convenience store. I simply had to have it. For years after that, *Playboy* was always my magazine of choice when it came to admiring gorgeous women. I liked that it didn't take things as far as other magazines. There was a taste and yes, even a certain class in how the photographers shot the models that appealed to me. Like most kids my age, yes, I got busted by my mom while I was masturbating one day in my bedroom. She would almost always knock before coming in, but this time she didn't. Maybe she had a hunch. "What are you doing?" she asked me. *Really,*

Masturbation

Mom? You can't see what I'm doing? I think it was more rhetorical than literal. But man, that took the steam out of things. I don't think I masturbated again until I started having sex a couple of years later.

School

When it came time to decide where I was going to attend junior high and high school, the choices didn't seem great. There was Walter Reed Middle School in North Hollywood, near where I lived, but we'd heard terrible stories about the initiation process there having to do with incoming seventh graders getting scrubbed down with metal wire brushes. I wanted no part of that, so I was admitted into Campbell Hall, a prep school in Studio City, even closer to our apartment. That didn't work out so well, either. The teachers would call my mom and say, "The girls are very distracted by your son. It's creating a problem here at school." Well, that was definitely true. My looks were starting to come together, I had appeared in a bunch of television shows, and so I think it was natural for a lot of the girls to pay attention to me. But the school also didn't like the fact that I was constantly leaving to go on auditions and interviews. So I left. Finally, I landed at a place called the Hollywood Professional School. This was a school designed for young actors that went back to the mid-1930s. It was located right on Hollywood Boulevard, and the legend is that MGM chief Louis B. Mayer was having such an issue with a thirteen-year-old actress at his studio named Judy Garland that he actually had somebody open a school for performers, a prep school that was open only until lunchtime to accommodate young actors' work hours. Everybody went there, from Betty Grable and Mickey Rooney to the cast of *The Brady Bunch*. When I was there I got to know Mackenzie Phillips, who was also a student. Interestingly, I wound up failing drama at this place. I have no idea why. I was a busy working actor, but some of the teachers there were kind of whacked-out and had their own impression of what acting really was. I believe the school shut down in 1984, but in fifty years it had acquired quite a legacy.

Three for the Road

I don't remember how I got cast in the TV show *Three for the Road*. I'm pretty sure I didn't even have to read for it and that it was basically given to me. The show was set to air on CBS in the fall of 1975. The premise involved a widowed father played by Alex Rocco. In the show, he and his two sons are so grief-stricken from the loss they are suffering collectively from the death of the wife/mother that the father decides to hit the road and travel around the United States with the boys. Pete Karras (the dad's name in the show) is a freelance writer and photographer always in search of new stories, so the constant road trips make sense. The eighteen-year-old son, John, was portrayed by Vincent Van Patten, and I played the thirteen-year-old, Endy. It was a cool show. What kid my age wouldn't love that sort of adventure, traveling all over and doing fun things? Our dad in the show purchases a large recreational vehicle nicknamed Zebec, which was the name of an old Mediterranean ship. We did thirteen episodes and shot all throughout the state of California. One of the most fun experiences for me was when I got to go hang-gliding in Monterey, California, in one of the episodes. We had some interesting guest stars, including Larry Hagman, Dean Stockwell, and Tim Matheson. It's a sweet show about a dad protecting his two sons by keeping them busy in the wake of their mother's death. The problem was, we were up against *The Wonderful World of Disney* on NBC and another family adventure show, *The Swiss Family Robinson*, on ABC. *Three for the Road* is a good show; it was well-produced, and I was dreaming about a second season because that would have allowed us to break out of California and actually travel around the country. The sixty-minute episodes were well-received critically but unfortunately didn't attract much of an audience. So much for all those great per diems I'd been getting on the road. As the show ended, we all said goodbye and I started thinking about what might be next in terms of my acting.

Then something happened that I never anticipated. Something that would change my life. Evidently, some of the teen magazines that were popular at the time had run some pictures of me when the show was on the air. The magazines were always looking for cute young faces, and I had appeared in a couple of them before, but it hadn't been a big deal. I certainly had never been on the cover of anything, nor had I generated much interest. But *Three for the Road* changed that. In September 1975, for the very first time, I was on the cover of *Tiger Beat* magazine. Then the show ended almost as quickly as it began. Yet even though it was off the air, the magazine kept getting lots of mail about me: literally duffel bags full of letters. The magazine had never seen that before. Usually for a young actor or singer to be generating lots of fan mail, he or she had to be in a current show. Yet long after *Three for the Road* was canceled, as the months went on and we entered early 1976, my mail kept going up and up and up. The editors had never seen anything like that before. That was strange. Something was up.

David MacLeod

My mom seems to remember him as a guy who discovered me at my school, the Hollywood Professional School. However he came into our lives, David MacLeod was definitely around a lot. He initially contacted my mom and said to her, "I'm Warren Beatty's cousin. Leif is a good actor, and he has a wonderful look." As with a lot of parents in Hollywood, this was music to my mom's ears, so much so that she probably overlooked the fact that he was a guy in his early thirties without any real credentials. But the mere fact that he was Beatty's cousin meant something. I mean, come on, this was 1975. The year *Shampoo* came out. Had the internet been invented at that point, it would've been easy to do some background checking on him. Perhaps then we would've discovered that he had been convicted of sexual crimes in his native country of Canada. But all we knew was that he seemed like a straight shooter and a normal enough guy, so he was allowed into our lives. It also helps to remember that my mom was always looking for ways to allow male influences in my life. Even though I wasn't thinking about father figures at that point (it would hit me much later in life), I think that was a good thing, but obviously she needed to be more selective in whom she let near me. It's a strange balance. I don't think for a moment my mom would ever have deliberately wanted to put me in harm's way. She loved me and my sister and cared for us very much. But I can't deny that there was also a blind spot that allowed for this sort of thing in the hope that maybe it could have advanced my career or given me a much-needed adult male role model.

Regardless, here was David MacLeod. He was shrewd. He understood me right away. He dressed well and presented himself well, and there was nothing threatening about him. He was very smart, cultured (spoke several languages fluently) and a good dresser in a casual, cool way. He would stop by and take me to the movies. He would take my family to dinner. He and I played racquetball (sometimes, in the locker room afterwards, he might be admiring his own body and say something like, "Not bad for a guy in his thirties, huh?"). David and I became friends. When he invited me to Warren Beatty's place high up on Mulholland Drive, it was cool. We would go up there, swim, hit some tennis balls on the court, and then soak in the Jacuzzi. Warren was never home when we were there except for one time when a chocolate-brown Mercedes-Benz pulled up to the house and out stepped the star himself.

As time went on, the only work I ever got from David was a voice-over role in the 1987 film, *The Pick-up Artist*. But I will admit I did get to do some interesting things with him. I remember I was in the Bay Area visiting my family a couple of years later, and he brought me to the set of *Heaven Can Wait*, which he was serving as an administrative associate on. Warren Beatty saw me, said "Hello" and we made some small talk. (We would run into each other occasionally over the years. One time in particular that stands out was around 1980 when we saw each other in a restaurant. By then I was dating Nicollette Sheridan; she was with me and I thought Warren would have a heart attack. I never noticed how much Nicollette looked like one of his first loves, Julie Christie, until he mentioned it to me that night.) They were shooting *Heaven Can Wait* at a beautiful mansion in Filoli gardens, in Woodside. At a distance, I saw the stunning Dyan Cannon, and I was reminded of that crazy schoolboy crush I'd had on her a few years earlier on the set of *Bob & Carol & Ted & Alice*.

David MacLeod was fun to hang out with. But he had secrets I would not learn about for many years.

Michael Lloyd: First Record

Sharon Lee, the editor of *Tiger Beat* magazine, contacted Michael Lloyd and suggested that he try getting me into a recording studio to capitalize on all of the mail and attention I was getting from the fans. Michael Lloyd was and is a very talented guy who, in addition to being a terrific songwriter and producer, also had a knack for helping to develop young talent into what I guess you could call teen idols. He had a stellar track record. In the 1960s, as a teenager, Michael had been a hotshot performer and producer working with many artists in Los Angeles. In 1970 he became vice president in charge of A&R (artists and repertoire) at MGM Records. While there, he helped craft and steer the careers of Lou Rawls and the Osmond Brothers, among many others. In 1975 he began working with Shaun Cassidy, and for the rest of Shaun's career, Michael did everything from produce his biggest records to lead Shaun's band onstage.

As much as anyone, Michael knew what it took to make a teen idol successful. So I got together with him, and I liked him. He was a funny guy who obviously knew a lot about the business, and he made me feel very comfortable as we recorded in his little home studio. A deal was struck with Twentieth Century Fox Records, and we did a cover song called "Come Back When You Grow Up," an old song by Bobby

Vee. I reflect a lot these days on my past lives, and this one for me will always kind of leave me scratching my head. Why was a fifteen-year-old singing "Come Back When You Grow Up"? Doesn't make sense to me, and the record-buying public didn't get it either. The single did nothing. So much for being a singer. I'll admit for one fleeting moment there I did kind of imagine myself as the next Robert Plant. I mean, what could be cooler than getting onstage in front of a huge adoring crowd and singing music? But it wasn't meant to be. At least not this time. Oh well. It was disappointing. At least I still had acting.

Israel

The year 1976, just before the teen idol thing came together, was busy for me, movie-wise. I shot *Skateboard,* and then it was off to Israel, of all places. I had been cast in a film produced by Menahem Golan and Yoram Globus, called *Kid Vengeance,* in which I starred with football legend Jim Brown, Lee Van Cleef, Glynnis O'Connor, and John Marley.

Living over there was an exotic experience. Jim Brown's son, Kevin, and I spent a lot of time together. Once we went exploring in a cave out in the Sinai desert, and we found a skull and bones. It was reported to the police, who came out to investigate, but I'm not sure what happened with it. It was brutally hot during the day out there, so we filmed a lot at night. My nose got broken over there (one of several times in my youth) because one of the extras didn't pull back his punch during a fight scene. It was fun working with such legendary actors over there even though it was grueling. This was the first time I had ever been out of the country, and it was a memorable place.

One day, late in the afternoon before it was time to shoot, I heard something outside my trailer. My trailer was farthest from the set and closest to the open desert. I think they put me all the way out there because of how loud I would crank my music. Jim Brown got me my first portable stereo while we were on location, and I used that thing to the fullest. But outside my trailer, there was a group of Israelis and some of the Italian crew, all huddled up in a circle. I went out there to see what was going on. Understand, oftentimes during a shoot you get pretty bored. I noticed that they had a broken Coca-Cola bottle that they had crafted into a glass pipe. Curiosity got the best of me. I asked, "What are you doing?" Gesturing with his hands at first, one of them tried explaining in broken English. "Smoking hashish—hash." As they passed the makeshift pipe around and took hits off of it, flames about five inches long would jump off the pipe. "Here," one of them said to me, "You try, you try." These were the crew guys that I worked every day with. I was just fourteen, but I wanted to be accepted. I wanted to be cool and hang out with these guys, so I carefully took the pipe when it was passed to me, listened to their directions about when to inhale the trapped smoke, and then I took a big hit. One of them said, "Hold it!" I tried, but I couldn't. I gagged and exhaled. The world started spinning like a top. I literally fell backward and hit my head on the desert floor. It was like being sucked into some vortex. I felt like I'd had the wind knocked out of me. I could hear the sounds as they all walked away from me, laughing. Well, that went great.

A few days later I was explaining what had happened to Jim Brown's son, Kevin, who was close to my age. He started laughing and said, "No wonder you felt sick. It was all that tobacco. That's not the right way to do it." He and I walked out into the desert away from everybody else's trailers and the set. Off behind some rocks he pulled out a piece of hash and put it on the sharp tip of a bent safety pin. "This is how you do it," he explained. He lit the gooey brown blob on the end of the pin, blew it out, and as it was glowing red, he covered it with a piece of glass to trap the smoke. He gave me the makeshift pipe and explained to me how to inhale gradually. Okay, this I kind of liked. This was a mellow high that actually felt good. And I felt a lot cooler than I did when I had arrived in Israel. I now knew how to get high.

After the film wrapped, I was asked to stay on and appear in another film the producers were shooting called *God's Gun*, featuring Lee Van

Cleef, Jack Palance, Sybil Danning, and Richard Boone. The problem was, they weren't going to start shooting for about two months and I wanted to go home. But that wasn't going to happen. I think they knew that if I went home to Los Angeles, there was no way I would come back. So they put a lot of pressure on me, paid me more money, and so we decided to stay. We wound up being in Israel for six months. My mom and sister were there the whole time with me. It wasn't that I didn't like it there. It was just too long. And there were little things. For instance, I loved cheeseburgers. But you can't get a cheeseburger there because it's not kosher to mix meat and dairy products. That may not seem like a big deal. But if you're fifteen years old and you've been away from home for months and you miss your friends and you miss your lifestyle back home (and your cheeseburgers), it all adds up. We made the most of the two months we had to kill. We visited all of the historic sites, like the Wailing Wall and many of the religious sites related to Jesus Christ. We were living in Eilat, Israel's southernmost city, which is a beautiful port and popular resort town on the northern tip of the Red Sea. We would drive to the desert almost every day. At the time, Eilat had just one hotel and this is where I learned how to drive. I had become friends with a French guy, the horse wrangler on location, and he took me water-skiing in Eilat, on the Gulf of Aqaba. We water-skied near the beautiful beaches and coral reefs. That is, until one day when we were followed by a large shark. That ended the water-skiing.

My mom and I would often go for walks at night in the Sinai desert. One evening something strange happened. We both looked into the sky and saw a strange series of lights flying together, moving stars. "Did you see that, Mom?" She didn't answer me, but she was staring at the sky and she nodded. I don't know what it was, but it did not seem of this Earth.

Soon, we'd be back home. Ready for the next adventure. Don't get me wrong, I loved Israel. The people were very warm and engaging, but six months in any place at that age would have driven me crazy. I was restless and homesick.

Losing My Virginity

In early 1977, my sister, mom, and I were back down in Jackson, Tennessee, for the production of *Final Chapter: Walking Tall*, the third and final installment in the *Walking Tall* film series. The third edition was directed by Jack Starrett, who was known as an actor for his role as Gabby Johnson in the hilarious film *Blazing Saddles*. Filming the *Final Chapter: Walking Tall* film was notable to me for two reasons: It was the first time I ever did cocaine, and it was also when I lost my virginity. Jack's daughter was visiting him on the set for most of the production, and I thought she was hot. Even though she was maybe only two years older than me, she felt much older and experienced (she definitely had experience sexually). She seemed to be interested in me too. One night, she and I were both hanging out in the first assistant director's hotel room. I could tell he had a thing for her too. She had to be used to it. She was so good-looking that I'm sure wherever she went, she broke hearts. That night the first assistant director took out a vial of cocaine and a small silver spoon. I was at a crossroads. I had never done coke before but didn't want to look like a little kid in front of her. Everybody else was doing it freely, and I wanted her to think that I was more mature than my age. For the first time in my life, I took the tightly rolled-up dollar bill and did my first couple of lines. The rush was immediate. I got why people like this stuff. It was scary though. It all went back to when I saw my cousin Peter smoking that first time. Even though I smoked pot pretty regularly now, cocaine scared me in the same way that I got scared when I first saw Peter get high. It seemed so serious. But I did it. Maybe I was imagining, but I could've sworn she looked at me in a way she was not looking at the first assistant director. I think she liked me.

The next night I asked her out on a date. There was a movie theater across the highway from the hotel, next to the roller rink where we'd sometimes go to skate during breaks in the shooting. At this movie theater, you could rent a private booth in the upper balcony, all to yourselves. I can't remember what it was I took her to see, but once we got up there in a little private space, I had what I considered to be my first authentic experience with a girl. I was so nervous. She took my hand in hers; I think she sensed what I was thinking. Somehow or other I got up the nerve to lean over and kiss her. And she opened her mouth. I'd never felt anything as hot as that before. It was the sexiest thing in the world. I absolutely loved the feeling. She slipped my hand in her blouse. She let me feel her. Then she whispered to me, "Let's get out of here and go back to the hotel." We crossed back over the highway together, holding hands and playfully kissing each other on the way back to her room. She and her dad were sharing a suite that had two separate bedrooms. We made sure that the door connecting the two rooms was locked.

When we fell into bed together, she resumed what she had been doing in the movie theater. That is, she was steering me through the process. She took my shirt off and she helped me take hers off as well. Soon we were both naked in the bed and as I positioned myself on top of her, she guided me. It was nerve-racking at first and I struggled a bit, but then all of a sudden I was inside of her. Okay. Wow. Now I understood. Now I got why this is what everybody wanted to do. It was the most incredible feeling in the world. The sheets were down below our waists. The phone next to the bed had been ringing, but we ignored it. All of a sudden, she looked toward the door as we both heard a sound, and then she quickly pushed me off of her. It was her father. He had been calling her, looking for her. The door leading into the room from the hallway evidently had not clicked shut when we got back from the movies. When he knocked on it, it had opened automatically. He had seen everything. I was dumbstruck. What did I do? What else? I pulled the covers over me and pretended like I wasn't there. There was a pause that lasted for an eternity. And then I heard her father, the director, simply say, "Hey, Leif, next time lock the door." And then he walked out.

To say that the rest of that shoot was awkward and uncomfortable would obviously be an understatement. But what a crush I now had on her.

Once I got back home to Studio City, she'd call me and we'd get together to finish what we had started in Tennessee. We both lived at home, so we'd rent cheap little motel rooms on Ventura Boulevard. I think the last time we were together, I hijacked my mom's new gold Cutlass (I had just gotten my learner's driving permit) to go see her. When I got home, my blissful postsex buzz was killed immediately by the sight of my mom, in the parking space, arms crossed and angrily tapping her foot. I was grounded for a time after this, thus killing any more escapes, at least for a while, with my first sexual partner. But my eyes were now wide open.

Led Zeppelin

David MacLeod said to my mom one day, "Carolyn, I want to take him to see Led Zeppelin at the Forum." "Oh, I think he would like that," my mom said. "And he has nobody else to do things like that for him. That's very kind of you." My mom was very trusting, but that led to a naïveté that could be dangerous. Of course, I know in hindsight that I never should've been going to a concert with David MacLeod. But go I did.

When he picked me up at our apartment, I noticed something outside—he wasn't driving his car. Instead there was a midnight-blue Jaguar parked out on the street. "I rented this for tonight," he said before handing me the keys. At that point, I had only a learner's permit. We got in the car, and the first thing he did was hand me a beer. And then he popped a Percocet. I cracked the bottle open, took a pill of my own, and we hit the road. Not long after I hit the 405 Freeway, he fired up a joint. I was a decent driver, but can you imagine what would've happened had we been pulled over? I was just fifteen years old.

When we got to the Forum, I parked the Jag and we headed in to the show. If you remember concerts in the mid-1970s, then you know how special that environment was. You could smell the dope in the haze of the arena as everybody got ready for what was one of the hottest shows that summer. Zeppelin was parked at the Forum for six nights that June. As much as I loved Elton John, the Zeppelin band members were my rock gods. I knew every note of every song on every album. David secretly cuffed a joint for us to pass back and forth as the lights went down and we heard the strains of "The Song Remains the Same." Jimmy Page looked resplendent in a white satin jumpsuit with bright green embroidered dragons running up the sides. Robert Plant was indeed the "Golden God," and the rhythm section of John Paul Jones and John Bonham was solid as ever and even more powerful live than on a record. This being one of my first concerts, it was absolutely incredible. I've always loved the combination of classical music and hard rock that Jimmy Page is known for, and seeing it live was unforgettable. I stood the entire time, thus pissing off some people behind me.

Back out in the parking lot of the Forum, we hurried back to the Jaguar to beat the traffic. David threw me back the keys and once again I was at the wheel, flying up the freeway toward my apartment. David had another idea. "Hey, before we take you home, I forgot, I have to pick up something at my place."

Back at his very typical 1970s bachelor pad, he grabbed us another couple of beers, fired up another joint, and dropped the needle down on side three of *Physical Graffiti*. Soon after, we hopped back in the Jaguar, and I drove us home. When I got inside, my mom called out from her bedroom, "Did you have a good time at the concert?" "Yeah, great," I called out over my shoulder as I went to the bathroom. I looked in the mirror. Man, I looked high. I climbed into bed, but not before firing up my own little stereo system and dropping "The Song Remains the Same" on.

Many of you may be wondering as you're reading this right now, what the hell was my mom thinking, letting this guy into our life? Trust me, I understand. I've wondered about it a lot myself, and I've also spoken to my mom a lot about it over the years. For a long time, situations like this caused a deep divide in our relationship. Obviously, it wasn't until I'd grown up and looked back at what happened to me that I began to have some serious questions about some of the judgment calls that she made. I'm not making excuses for my mom. She has apologized to me over the years for the way she handled certain things, and I've accepted her apologies. She is my mom, after all. I loved her then, I love her now, and I will always love my mom. But yes, obviously, I had many questions about what she had been thinking.

Another thing to consider, which is definitely part of my mom's story, is that as I have written here in this book, she was raised in an environment in which women simply were not supposed to speak up. That was part of her background. She would rarely challenge any male because she had been taught that that was not okay. And another component that factors into this entire mess is that she genuinely did want me to have some male influences in my life. Truth be told, David MacLeod seemed like an okay guy for the most part. I always had a great time playing racquetball with him, he was into good music, and I'm also pretty sure that in the back of her head my mom was hoping he could do something to advance my career. All of these factors contributed to the fact that I was not protected against people like this. There are other moments in my life you will hear about later when this same thing happened. My mom and I had some tough times over the years as I came to grips with my upbringing. In my head, I came to understand what I believe went into some of her decisions. But I also believe that our relationship is a private matter and it's complicated, just like many child-parent relationships are.

Shaun's Loss, My Gain

It's amazing how much of my life is about being in the right place at the right time. Michael Lloyd, who had worked on my first single the year before, was working very closely with Shaun Cassidy. Shaun was starring in a TV show, *The Hardy Boys* (which I had auditioned for). In one of the episodes, it was dictated by the network that Shaun was to sing the old Beach Boys tune "Surfin' USA." He did, and there was a huge reaction from the fans demanding that he release it as a record. But Shaun didn't want to do that. He didn't feel like it fit him. Michael Lloyd agreed, and Michael, ever the shrewd star maker, remembered my little surfer dude persona. At least, that's what he thought of me. That's when the idea was hatched. That was the spark of what became my teen idol career. Even though my first record had bombed, Michael now approached me again with the idea that I talk to his friends, the Scotti brothers, about doing that song and, eventually, an entire album. They were looking at me as the next teen idol. They were aware that I was still popular in the magazines, and all of a sudden, it seemed to be the perfect recipe. The perfect storm.

Peter Lundy

Peter Lundy and the Medicine Hat Stallion was simply one of the most fun things I ever did on television. It took two months to film, and I loved every second of it. It was shot in New Mexico, and the fact that I could ride horses every day made it special. It was filmed at the Dunigan Ranch in Los Alamos. Interestingly, the ranch had been used only once before for a film: in 1971 when my sister starred with Gregory Peck in a film called Shoot Out.

I played Peter Lundy, a fifteen-year-old boy growing up in pre–Civil War Nebraska Territory with my father, Jethro (played by Mitchell Ryan); my mother, Emily (played by Bibi Besch); and Grandma Lundy (played by Ann Doran). In the story, I resent the tyrannical way my father treats me, and I hate the bleak life we're living on our prairie trading post. I raise a foal that was left at the trading post as a payment; when it becomes old enough to ride, I win a job with the Pony Express to carry correspondence and messages between the East and West Coasts. It's a rough, hard job, but I do it and earn the respect of my father. If only life had imitated this art.

The made-for-TV movie would eventually be awarded the Bronze Wrangler for Outstanding Western Fictional Television Program by the National Cowboy & Western Heritage Museum, and I also had the honor of being inducted into the Cowboy Hall of Fame.

This may be the most fun I ever had on a production. The ranch was simply gorgeous. It was huge, privately owned, and I became friends with the ranch owners and their two sons, who were close to my age. Whenever I had free time, we would ride dirt bikes all across the land and then trade the bikes in for horses. There were endless rolling fields and lots of trees to climb, and for a curious and athletic kid like me, it didn't get any better.

I had my own room at this great little motel located in the middle of nowhere—one of those classic ranch-style places that has a kidney-shaped swimming pool, and we were surrounded by natural hot springs that were always fun to escape to. It was paradise. It was also a fairly long shoot, a couple of months, which for a movie of the week is a lot of time. And the per diem was one of the highest I had ever received. As well, I loved the cast. I was an actor at heart, and these were the experiences I enjoyed most. In terms of timing, this was right before the teen idol thing took off. Once it did, I was disappointed that I didn't get to go to the Cowboy Hall of Fame induction ceremony, which happened as a result of this film, but I was already on the road as a teen idol. I would much rather have been in Oklahoma to receive that award.

Back Up North: Moonlight

I was up in Sausalito one more time before things started getting crazy. As usual, Peter and all of my cousins and friends were hanging out. We'd been working on the boats for a couple of weeks and spending a lot of time on the water racing and screwing around. It was the best. My aunt and uncle also had a cabin in the redwoods, and that was fantastic too. On the water, we would race twelve-foot-long Spitfire boats built for two people. We had such a ball. But as much as I loved the water, my favorite place up there was a fire road that we would ride our bikes down from Mount Tamalpais. Up in the woods, a steep dirt road all to ourselves—it was the ultimate feeling of freedom mixed with youthful, reckless abandon. On that last trip up there before things got crazy back down in LA, we were cruising down the fire road, out of control. Peter lost the chain on his bike and flew past me, but somehow he still managed to hang on. Under a full moon I rode down that dirt trail, whooping it up into the night. Like the trail ahead, barely illuminated by the moonlight, what lay ahead in my life was something I could not even imagine.

Part Two

DURING

The Scotti Brothers

My mom and I first met Tony and Ben, the Scotti brothers, at their offices on Sunset Boulevard. Tony was impressive: handsome and charismatic. He'd been a football star at the University of Maryland but ended up in New York City, where he became an actor and a singer. In the 1967 film *Valley of the Dolls*, Tony portrayed Sharon Tate's character's love interest, Tony Polar. He also sang in the film and appears on the film's soundtrack. But in 1971, he stopped working as an actor and entered the record business as part of the production department at MGM. While there, he worked with Donny and Marie Osmond, Tony Bennett, Lou Rawls, Petula Clark, Sammy Davis Jr., and many others. In 1974, he and his brother, Ben, formed a public relations company that represented lots of artists, including Barbra Streisand, Bob Dylan, Bette Midler, John Denver, and the band Foreigner.

I could tell my mom was impressed by Tony. And why not? To me, he had warmth and charisma and right away made us feel like, well, family. That's what he told us. "We want you to feel like family here. That's how we do business, just like family. Let's not even think about this so much as business as it is family." That should have been a bright red alarm right there. I mean, Tony was a nice guy. He made an incredible impression, and he won my mom over right away. Me too, for that matter. But looking back, do you want to be doing business with your family?

Ben Scotti was different. A former professional football player, Ben always struck me as Tony's "enforcer." He was thug-like to me, the guy who took care of business behind the scenes while Tony charmed everyone out front.

Everything started happening pretty quickly. Without thinking too much about it, I signed a five-year management deal with the Scotti brothers. As managers, they would obviously get a percentage of everything I did, just like my lawyer, my publicist, my personal manager, my business manager, my theatrical agent...everybody got a piece. I can't tell you how much I wish we had known a little bit more about the business at this point. My mom went along with it, as did I. We had stars in our eyes. But nobody in our corner. It was times like those when having a real "protector" in the house would have made a difference. Somebody to step in and say, "Wait a minute. We're not signing anything until we examine it closely." But that's not what happened. We didn't ask questions.

According to my contract, or whatever dictated these terms, I would not ever receive any kind of monthly salary or hourly wage or lump sum; I would get money only when I requested it. I'm not blaming the Scotti brothers. This is on me and my family. We never asked to audit any books, never made sensible inquiries as to the status of whatever money I was making. If I wanted a car, I bought a car. If I wanted clothes, I asked for money. It was that cut and dried, as crazy as it sounds. In my head, there was a bank where I could go withdraw endless money and everything would be okay. I kick myself very hard about it today, but I also take full responsibility.

The Scottis had a plan to get me signed to Atlantic Records because, as they saw it, teen idols had a hard time getting records on the radio unless they had some credibility. Atlantic Records provided just the kind of pedigree to make me seem more appealing to radio programmers. I mean, that was the plan anyway. We met at the Scotti brothers' offices on Sunset Boulevard, signed the contracts, and then, soon after that, I met Bob Greenberg at the Atlantic offices in Los Angeles. Both my mom and I loved Bob. The folks at the Atlantic office were terrific.

Being on Atlantic Records was a double-edged sword. On the one hand, it was stunning to me that I was sharing a label with my heroes: Led Zeppelin, the Rolling Stones, and many others. On the other hand, it was incomprehensible that somebody who had paid zero musical dues could actually be part of such an elite and storied musical family. That constantly played a part in my emotions. *I'm not worthy of this; I have no business being on Atlantic with all of these legends.* And yet it was happening. So why resist or fight the feelings of excitement? My brain was constantly torn over this dilemma. I wanted so badly to actually pay my dues and carve out my own musical identity. Atlantic may have been the perfect place to do that, given its history. They were known for nurturing and developing young artists. But I wasn't allowed to change anything. The Scotti brothers picked the songs. They designed the covers. They directed every single aspect of what I did, and Atlantic fell in line with them. The Scotti Brothers, I'm sure, made Atlantic aware that they simply had a distribution deal for me. It wasn't about getting me A&R support to help me grow; the Scotti brothers had everything covered. And so whenever I was in the presence of other Atlantic artists, whether it was backstage at a Foreigner concert or actually getting the chance to meet Robert Plant, I felt like I didn't deserve to be there. I knew the truth. And the truth was killing me.

Teen Magazines

Tiger Beat magazine was founded in September 1965 by Charles Laufer, the Los Angeles–based founder of *Teen* magazine. Originally a journalism and English teacher at Beverly Hills High School, Laufer imagined that a magazine devoted to teen obsessions would be a success. In the 1950s he created *Coaster*, a magazine for teens based in Long Beach, California. Eventually, he renamed the magazine *Teen*, and it became a success. From there he created *Tiger Beat*. His timing could not have been better. The Monkees had just been introduced, and Laufer realized he could do more than just sell magazines featuring the band. He also sold fan club memberships, posters, books, and more.

Laufer thoroughly understood the need for a magazine that was devoted to rising young stars from all walks of entertainment: TV, film, fashion, music, sports, theater—everything. The *Tiger Beat* target audience was primarily female, ages ten to nineteen. *Tiger Beat* also featured a variety of spinoffs, including *FaVE*, *Tiger Beat Spectacular*, and *Tiger Beat Star*. There were special issues dedicated to the Monkees and the Partridge Family; eventually there would even be a special "Leif Garrett Photo Album."

Tiger Beat's trademarks included bright and colorful covers and pinups (posters that girls would pin up on their bedroom walls). The magazine was located at 7060 Hollywood Boulevard, and it was an address I would soon become quite familiar with.

Tiger Beat was far from the first teen idol magazine. New York–based *16 Magazine* was launched in 1957, and around the world there were many others, including *Patches, Mates, Oh Boy!, Jackie, Look-in* (all in the UK), and Germany's popular *Bravo*. But early in my career, *Tiger Beat* was the first one that truly mattered. Charles Laufer was at first surprised by my popularity because of his experience: Blonds never made a big splash in the magazines. But there I was getting more mail than anyone. Also, the rule of thumb was that it was virtually impossible to start a fan club for someone who didn't have a series. Nevertheless, Laufer started my fan club in 1976 after my series *Three for the Road* was dropped. He stated back then, "Leif's drawing more mail than John Travolta, who has a series." He then offered, "Leif is not only drawing more mail than John Travolta, but also more than the Bay City Rollers and Donny and Marie. Leif has virtually no exposure at all—yet his fan mail remains steady. This is unprecedented in company history." When I first started going to the *Tiger Beat* offices—about once a week—they would usually give me little questionnaires to fill out, answering questions. What was I looking for in a girlfriend? What was my favorite food? Stuff like that. A lot of it was innocent, but some of it actually seemed inappropriate in terms of how they wove adult subject matter into the seemingly innocent pages. It wasn't just about winning a dream date with me. It was about becoming my wife, wanting to have kids with me; it was strange. One issue literally featured a board game where you would go around the board trying to wind up as my wife. I would sit and patiently answer questions and then prepare for a long day of having my picture taken. I would typically bring along a bunch of different clothes to change in and out of, and I would pose on the set for their house photographer, Kenny Lieu.

The editors were brilliant with how they created the images that they did. I rarely had a clue as to what they were up to. They would create all of these weird story lines and narratives, and I never knew about them unless I picked up a magazine and saw that they were advertising what I wanted in a wife or what it would take for someone to spend the rest of her life with me. It's not like anybody ever sat down and talked to me about those things. All they needed from me were more pictures. Lots and lots of pictures. For the exterior shots, they would usually buy those from somebody like Barry Levine or Neil Zlozower or Brad Elterman. They rarely did location shoots. Instead, I would sit in a studio for hours striking pose after pose, looking at the camera, pouting or smiling or doing whatever they told me to. I took direction well. Hey, I was an actor. There wasn't that much to it. The way I looked was the way I looked.

As the magazine covers continued (and I want to tell you, to this day I have a copy of every single one of those magazines thanks to my mom, who collected and saved everything), the mail bags got heavier and heavier. Each day there were numerous duffel bags—each about four and a half feet high—waiting at the post office. When all of this had started, I would diligently sit and try to answer every letter. I would sign every picture, and I considered that part of my responsibility. But when you're talking thousands of letters a day, well, there was only so much time in the day. I hate to admit it, but there was soon a small army of people who would sit and sign my name to pictures and letters and send them back to little girls all over the world. I think my mom had my signature down best. I'll see autographs today at auctions and things like that, and I know for a fact I did not sign them. But what embarrassed me was when I was on the road and a girl would come up to me and say, "Oh, Leif, thank you so much for writing me back, and I loved that little message!" and I knew I had done no such thing. So I would smile and nod and say, "You're welcome," and move on. It was all part of the act. It was all part of the charade. That's what made this so different than acting. As an actor, I had to learn my lines and I had to go out there and perform. There were no shortcuts, and I liked that. I was responsible for my performance. As a teen idol, I felt like it was the exact opposite. All I had to do was look pretty.

Tiger Beat set up my official fan club. Were any of you members? What would you get for $5.50 per year? To quote *Tiger Beat*:

- A 45 RPM record in Leif's own voice with a very special personal message for you.
- A life-size 16 x 22 full color poster of Leif Garrett.
- 9 wallet-size photos of your favorite—each one completely different!
- A hand-written message from Leif.
- A 16-page fact-filled booklet all about Leif featuring: 51 of Leif's favorite things, 15 "First Facts" from Leif... Are you his type? Leif speaks out!
- Over five dozen Leif stickers for your mirror, notebooks, letters—Let everyone know Leif is your favorite.
- Your official Leif Garrett Fan Club Membership Card.
- Your official Leif Garrett Decoder to translate the very personal message Leif sends you in every message of *Tiger Beat*.
- Join Today! Let Leif know you love him!

Brad Elterman

As I said, I got to work with a lot of great photographers when the magazines were interested in me. But the guy I worked with the most, and became good friends with, was Brad Elterman. Brad was great. The very first time he came over to our apartment in Studio City, he made me feel relaxed. He was cool. He was only a few years older than me, so right away he was different than most of the other photographers—all of whom were a good deal older. Brad never pressured me, and I thought he always had good ideas. He didn't shoot just for teen magazines. As a teenager himself, he'd begun photographing musicians all over Los Angeles. He caught some classic images of David Bowie, Robert Plant, Bob Dylan, and many others. He was always in the right place at the right time, and whether he was shooting Joan Jett when she was still in the Runaways in some seedy little Hollywood motel, or Steve Jones of the Sex Pistols in the swimming pool at his house, Brad always got great captures. He was creative and artistic.

A couple of years after we met, Brad traveled on the road with me, and we had some wonderful adventures together. But early on, he helped me become comfortable in front of the camera. When I saw his pictures of me in the teen magazines, I knew they were better than a lot of the others because I was more comfortable and relaxed. That was the key with me. When I was comfortable, then I behaved and I gave you what you needed. But make me uncomfortable and I could shut down. My mom and sister also liked Brad and were always happy when he came over to our little apartment. He made everybody comfortable; he was funny and fun to be around. In a way, the "Leif Garrett look" is partially due to Brad's careful eye. He chose great locations and always made sure to get images of me that nobody else did. His shots were always very distinctive, personal, and even intimate at times. Soon, he would shoot arguably the most famous picture ever taken of me. But we'll get to that story in just a bit. I consider myself lucky that this was a guy I had bonded with early because in a world that was getting increasingly blurry and crazy, he always provided a calm, eye-of-the-storm vibe that I always looked forward to. I'm glad we're still friends today.

Atlantic Records

The Scotti brothers knew Atlantic Records had never had a teen idol on its label, and they figured Atlantic would provide all of the credibility to get someone like me played on regular rock 'n' roll radio. It was a risk for sure, but I'm glad they took it. After all, Atlantic Records was the home of Led Zeppelin and the Rolling Stones, not to mention many other legendary rock 'n' roll, rhythm and blues, and jazz artists. I honestly couldn't believe they signed a deal with Atlantic. What had I done to deserve this kind of notoriety on a label like this? I hadn't paid any dues. This was the beginning of the insecurity I started feeling as someone who had never, ever sung before. Why would Atlantic hire somebody who could not sing? The Scottis were good salesmen, obviously. And they had convinced Atlantic I would be good for some hit records.

After I met Bob Greenberg at the Atlantic office in Los Angeles, we soon flew to New York and met his brother—the president of the label—Jerry Greenberg and, of course, Ahmet Ertegun. The Greenbergs were both incredible men: down-to-earth and very likeable. Ertegun was the founder of Atlantic, a Turkish immigrant, an elegant and dynamic man whose charms totally won over my mom and me. We had a big signing ceremony in which pictures were taken because, back then, everything I did was merely for the sake of a photo op. This was the big time.

Standing in the boardroom signing a contract, I started thinking, *Hey, maybe this is the start of my career as a real rock star.* Of course, I barely even knew what I was signing. My mom and I were so happy and excited that we didn't think too hard about what exactly it was we were getting involved with. This was the story of our lives. Like many other artists, we just signed on the line and thought all good things would follow. We were "family," right? I was just happy to now be a rock star in training. Maybe I could take singing lessons and maybe—just maybe—I could get good. I truly thought I was going to get good. I thought, *Maybe I'll even write some songs once in a while, or maybe I'll be able to choose material that I like and feel comfortable with.* That's what I thought it took to be a real rock star: You couldn't just have the look and be a poser. You had to back it up with the songs. All the bands I loved, no matter how cool they may have looked, had what I considered to be the greatest singers in the world. That's what I wanted to be. I want to be a great rock 'n' roll singer. That's how I approached my acting, even at an early age; I always wanted to learn, and I always wanted to get better. I always tried to apply myself, and my directors liked that. I assumed that this would also be the right approach to singing—that I could be myself and do whatever it took to get better and that I would get support in those efforts.

I could not have been more wrong.

The First Album

I didn't know what to expect when I went in to record my first album. I had been in the recording studio a couple of times but didn't have a lot of experience. What surprised me at first was the fact that I was brought in once the musical tracks had, for the most part, already been created. It wasn't like I was working in a band situation. Everything basically had already been done by talented studio musicians by the time I walked in, and I just had to sing the songs in the proper key. Well, that was a bit of an issue. I wasn't a singer. But Michael Lloyd was good at coaching me and helping me at least get through enough takes so that there would be something usable once they got down to editing. Of course, it wasn't like my voice was going to be front and center. Through the magic of production, it was doubled, tripled—even quadrupled—and processed to the point where it barely sounded like me at all.

It was me singing on the records, but not just me alone, doubled or not. There was a well-known and very accomplished background singer named Jim Haas whom Michael had brought in to sing on the sessions. The thing was, his voice was very prominent. He was a strong singer, and at times I felt like we were in there making his record as opposed to mine. Right away that made me feel kind of funny. What's it going to be, me singing on a record or not? Granted, these were not songs I had any real interest in recording. For the most part they were cover tunes, including "The Wanderer," "California Girls," "Put Your Head on My Shoulder," "Johnny B. Goode," "Runaround Sue," "Surfin' USA," and even the old Nat King Cole standard "That's All." What the hell? I was sixteen years old, and those were the songs that I would be singing? The Scottis obviously were pulling a page from the playbook of "once a hit, always a hit," and no chances were being taken. These old standards, plus the dominance of Jim Haas's singing, set me on the course of believing I wasn't a real singer. I understood that nobody on the outside would ever notice that my voice wasn't at all prominent. They would assume, naturally, that if my face was on the album cover, I was the singer. But watching Jim Haas dominate the sessions, I knew the truth. This was not really my record. Maybe that wasn't even the point. It was about my look, not my sound. And that's not what I wanted. What exactly had I bargained for here?

After the record was done and mastered, we shot a couple of music videos, including one for "Surfin' USA" out on the beach in Oxnard on the way to Santa Barbara. I remember saying to them at one point back then, "Imagine a TV channel where all they did was play music videos. People my age would love that." The answer? "Shut up, kid. We'll do the thinking." A year or so later, "Hello, MTV."

The album did well. There were four singles: "Surfin' USA," which made it to number two in Australia and to the top twenty in America; "Runaround Sue," which made it to number thirteen on the US charts; "Put Your Head on My Shoulder;" and "The Wanderer." All four singles were cover songs of former hits from another era. I was simply doing a note-for-note remix, and the Scotties were right; I guess a hit was a hit was a hit. The Scotti brothers told me they had loved these songs when they were my age. I wasn't that familiar with these songs, nor did I even like them, but that didn't matter. What mattered was selling records. And I was doing that. The album went gold in a number of countries, and I remember the very first ceremony when I was presented with my first gold record. I was staring closely at it, and something seemed strange. I examined the actual record very closely, and it had more songs in the grooves than were actually listed on the label. I asked my manager about it, and he said, "Oh, they don't actually use your record when they make a gold one. They just take whatever's lying around." Nothing was real, it seemed.

The First U.S. Promotional Tour

In the summer of 1977, when I was still fifteen, Tony Scotti sat me and my mom down and laid out what the plan was for the next several months: basically, lots of travel and lots of promotional appearances. That was the strategy. No real concerts or anything; it was all about radio appearances, mall tours, and generally trying to capitalize on the excitement generated by the teen magazines. That was my audience. They wanted those girls who waited each week for new pictures of me to come out and see me in the flesh. My job was basically to look good, smile, be friendly, sign autographs, and move on, from city to city. Accompanying me on this first major road trip was going to be Tony's brother, Ben, and another one of my Scotti brothers handlers, Craig Dudley. We would be heading east—starting off down South in Florida and Atlanta and working our way up the coast to upstate New York, then back down the coast again to Florida. We would hit as many major markets as we could, and the real goal was to try to get the record played at radio stations. I was told we would visit with radio programmers and promo guys and that it would be an exciting time for me.

I felt like I was growing up fast. It was going to be weird not having somebody my own age—or even my mom or any family—traveling with me. I wasn't sure I was comfortable hitting the road with two grown men, but this evidently was going to be my new life. My mom and I were both excited at the idea of my being a rock star, but I'm not quite sure we thought through the way it was all going to shake out. I had been acting long enough that I understood that part of the business. I was fairly seasoned. But this was all totally new for me.

Our first stop was Atlanta, and it gave me a taste of what the next few years were going to be like. As was reported in a local Atlanta newspaper after my first appearance, "Lots of little female hearts beating faster this weekend because Leif Garrett was visiting Atlanta. Leif, for those who haven't heard, is a superstar of fan magazines, a 15-year-old actor with a full decade of experience behind him and, most immediately, the spark plug behind a hit recording. His rendition of the old rock 'n' roll tune, 'Surfin' USA,' has moved onto the popularity charts with spectacular speed. The song broke into the top 100 after only one week and release, which is quite difficult because of the tabulation process. Now after two weeks and release, the tune has moved even higher in the rankings."

Wherever we went in Atlanta, from record stores to shopping malls, the crowds got bigger and bigger, and clearly something was happening there. It struck me just how powerful those magazines were. This was not because of the music; it was because of publications like *Tiger Beat*. That's what was drawing the young girls out.

I think I was doing a pretty good job of dealing with the crowds and the attention and being a nice, polite kid with all of the radio programmers, but I didn't like traveling with Ben Scotti. He struck me as kind of a thug. He had a foul mouth and always seemed to be bullying the people we met at the radio stations. In one of the cities (it may have been Boston), I was headed back down to the car with Craig, but realized I had forgotten my jacket in the studio. I went back up there and saw Ben yelling at the guy—practically threatening him to play the new record. I couldn't believe that's how business was getting done. Ben stormed out of the studio and I went back in there, meekly, to apologize for what I'd witnessed. I said to the guy, "Look, do what you have to do; play the record or don't play the record, but I'm really sorry you had to go through that." For years to come I'd end up playing that part: apologizing for the behavior of adults around me, whether they were too drunk, too stoned, or just hell-bent on breaking knee-caps to get my new album played.

Magic Mountain

When we got back from the first PR tour, it was time for my first real public concert performance, if you can call it that. I had been flying all over the country, visiting radio stations to do interviews and try to get the record played while also going to shopping malls to brave mobs of shrieking young girls who wanted my autograph.

September 23, 1977. This was it. I was booked to appear at Magic Mountain, an amusement park located just outside of Los Angeles. I had been there before, like a lot of other kids my age. But this was going to be different. I wasn't going there to ride roller coasters and stuff my face with carnival food while checking out pretty girls. Instead, I arrived with the people from the Scotti brothers' office and, once through the front gates, we made a quick and hurried beeline to the stage door of the theater. (If you're a fan of the movie *This Is Spinal Tap*, you might remember the venue as the place where the band played when they had a puppet show opening up for them—when things started to go south.)

There was a small backstage area, and through a black velvet curtain I kept stealing little glimpses. The place was absolutely packed. I stepped closer to the curtain, peeked through, and saw hundreds of young girls, many of them holding homemade signs and banners with my name emblazoned on them.

I still wasn't quite sure what was going on. I had been told that this was going to be my first concert. When we got there, I asked one of my managers, "Is there going to be a band playing behind me?" "No, kid. There's going to be a black curtain behind you. That's your band." All of the adults started laughing when he said that. Then he told me, "All you need to do is get out there and lip-synch the song. 'Surfin' USA' is going to start playing over the public address system, and all you need to do is to pretend to be singing it. You'll be fine."

I was scared out of my mind. This wasn't the kind of performing I had any experience with. I was an actor. They were going to give me a microphone that wasn't even turned on and just have me lip-synch the song? I had been to a number of concerts already. I had seen Crosby, Stills, Nash & Young. I had seen Led Zeppelin and the Rolling Stones at the Forum. I knew what a concert was supposed to be like. I knew how a concert was supposed to feel. And this was not going to be that. I peeked out again, and the crowd had gotten even larger. I saw girls wearing T-shirts with my face on it. This wasn't even my show. There was a band called the Sylvers who was the headliner, and I was merely the warm-up. But you never would've known that by looking at the crowd. I was wishing I had some alcohol. I needed something to numb my nerves. When I had been approached about making a record, I never thought about this part of it. I never thought about what performing would be like. Nobody had coached me or given me any direction. I was simply being thrust out there to the lions to see what would happen.

A few moments later, a stage manager tapped me on the shoulder and said, "You're on, kid. Get out there." I was hastily pushed out in front of the curtain, and a roar of high-pitched screaming erupted, washing over me like a sonic wave. I remembered seeing a documentary in which John Lennon was talking about playing at Shea Stadium with the Beatles. He said that the screaming was so loud, they didn't even need to be singing. That they could have started yelling, "Blah

blah blah blah blah" into the microphones and nobody would have noticed. All of a sudden, I knew exactly what he was talking about. I heard "Surfin' USA" starting over the loudspeakers, and I did what they had told me to: I started lip-synching the song. I didn't move around that much; I basically stood there and sang—or rather, pretended to sing. What's funny is, as an actor, I had done a lot of ADR, or automated dialogue replacement. These were looping sessions in which an actor is required to match dialogue to action on the screen, re-performing the words so they fit with the image. This had made me a decent lip-syncher.

As I kept mouthing the words, the screams reached an even higher fever pitch. It was an outright frenzy. I was thinking, *I don't even like this song.* I was a huge music fan, but I wasn't into surf music—no offense to the Beach Boys. It just wasn't my thing. Also, the song had a slow fade-out as opposed to a hard ending. How do you deal with a slow fade-out when you are lip-synching? Awkwardly, that's how. I finished the song, and the screams grew even louder. I wasn't sure what to do, but I assumed I was finished, so I sheepishly gave the crowd a little wave and headed for the wings. Not so fast. I saw my management team huddled up over there, and they were all motioning for me to stay on the stage. The stage manager called out to me, "Do it again! They want you to do it again!" What? Before I could even consider what was going on, the song started over again and I repeated my lip-syncing performance. If it was even possible at that point, the crowd got crazier. Once the song ended again, I was ordered to do it one more time. And once again, the screaming got even more intense. At the end of my performance, the emcee, the well-known deejay Machine Gun Kelly from KHJ radio came out and yelled happily to the hyperventilating mob, "How about it, girls? Do we love Leif Garrett?" Behind me, as I left the stage, it sounded as if a full-scale riot might be breaking out.

Looking back, I think this was the moment that I sold my soul. This wasn't a concert. This was a concoction. My handlers off to the side were so excited when I left the stage, patting me on the back, tousling my hair, and telling me how great I had done. "The kid is a natural! He can't miss!" But I hadn't done anything. I had stood up there and pretended to sing a song I didn't even like. There was nothing real about it. But that didn't matter. A few days later, we headed up to Oxnard and a crew shot a promotional videotape of me lip-synching "Surfin' USA." I basically took a surfboard and ran down to the water a couple of times and met up with some girls. A few days later, I was back at the offices of *Tiger Beat* magazine, answering even more questions about my favorite foods, where I liked to travel, and what I looked for in a woman. That first test of lip-synching onstage, I had evidently passed with flying colors. If I'd only known the costs.

Sweet Sixteen

In anticipation of my sixteenth birthday, The Laufer Company (which published *Tiger Beat*) threw me a big birthday party on its yacht. The party served a couple of purposes. One, it allowed the company bigwigs to express to me and my family just how important they felt I was to their magazines. But, of course, it also gave them an opportunity to have photos of me taken to be used as features in the very pages of those magazines. At that point in my life, it felt like every single move I made was being photographed for some ulterior motive. When I woke up. When I brushed my teeth. When I combed my hair. When I got behind the wheel of a car. When I skateboarded. When I swam. When I walked my dog. When I sneezed. No action was so slight that it couldn't be developed into some kind of a photo feature for the magazines. Before the party, one of my managers, Stan, told me, "You need to be on good behavior. This is a real honor. You need to go and stroke these people. We want to keep them on our side. Do you realize how many magazine covers this one party will probably result in?" Precocious teenager that I was, however, I did manage to find a way to screw things up, at least to some degree. I had a buddy named Dana Kershner who lived near us. His dad, Irv, was a well-known director who would eventually go on to direct *The Empire Strikes*

Back). Anyway, I invited Dana to come to the party with me. He and I both planned on smoking weed at the party so I brought some along. We thought we were clever when we went down below, on the yacht, closed ourselves in the bathroom to smoke, and opened the window. I guess we didn't realize that the smoke was going to blow back to the rear deck where everybody was sitting. When we emerged back up on deck I could tell my mom was miffed. "What's the matter?" I asked her, eyes all glazed. "We can smell everything up here," she hissed under her breath. I felt badly, but then again, everybody was sitting up on deck getting drunk so how terrible was what we were doing? One of many times that always being around adults got in the way.

Still, the people at The Laufer Company were all pretty cool, and they threw a great event for me. We had an amazing lunch on their yacht, and then they presented me with a forty-five horsepower Mercury motor for my speedboat that I kept up in the Bay Area near my cousin, Peter, and the rest of my family. They gave me other presents as well and were very kind to my mom and sister. The head of the company, Charles Laufer, made a very nice speech about me and about how much he felt that I meant to their publications. I also received my first credit card for my birthday: a gold American Express card (which was as exclusive as it got in 1977). I had also just got my license and so I went out and leased my first car, a killer green Fiat 124 Sport Spider.

And the parties did not end on the yacht. The Scotti brothers threw me a very nice surprise party, which I screwed up by coming in the back door, thus spoiling the entire surprise. Then my mom threw me a party at the Sportsmen's Lodge in Los Angeles, with a disco dinner theme. I guess I was pretty spoiled. But it was a wonderful time in life. We actually celebrated my birthday a few days early because I was slated to go to Europe for my first overseas promotional tour. When I arrived there, the German magazine *Bravo* threw me yet another sweet sixteen birthday extravaganza.

The First European Promotional Tour: London Hotel

Before heading over to the UK for my first European promotional tour, I did a number of TV appearances in the States, including my very first shot on *American Bandstand*, singing "Surfin' USA" and "Special Kind of Girl." It was a real thrill to meet Dick Clark, and as I got to know him over the years, appearing on the show a number of times, he was never anything less than very gracious and kind with me. I had always watched the show as a kid, and it was surreal to be out there on that stage and having him come over to talk to me after I was done lip-synching.

And then it was time to get on a plane for my big trip. I had no idea what to expect. We'd heard the record was doing pretty well in Europe, and all I would be doing was visiting radio stations and appearing on TV shows to lip-synch "Surfin' USA." We were going to start in London and then work our way through Spain and Germany. Traveling with me would be Stan Moress. My mom had tears in her eyes the day I left: November 6, 1977. Her birthday. Two days before my sixteenth birthday. This was a big deal. It was starting to feel as if this music thing was going to be pulling me away from and affecting my family. But that's just how it was. I was nervous, but it was a good kind of nervous. It was an adventure.

I was actually starting to feel famous at this point, but nothing prepared me for the Dorchester Hotel in London. It's one of the world's most prestigious and expensive hotels, a five-star luxury extravaganza. And it has so much history. Many famous writers and artists, such as Cecil Day-Lewis and W. Somerset Maugham, stayed here. Elizabeth Taylor and Richard Burton also frequently stayed there. It is located right by Hyde Park and was one of the prettiest buildings I'd ever seen. After we checked in, it got even better. We were not staying in just any room; we had booked the exquisite Terrace suite. This was where royalty and heads of state would stay. And now it was mine? What did this thing cost? Obviously, money was no object to the Scotti brothers. They wanted to take good care of me because, after all, I was "family," remember? I unpacked my bags and began wandering around the enormous suite. I had never been in any place that had even approached having this kind of grandeur.

After the long flight, I was hungry, and I picked up the phone to order room service. Several moments later, there was a knock at the door and my own private chef came in. What? All I was in the mood for was maybe a scrambled egg or something. But the chef was prepared to make me whatever I felt like. He had actually taken a private elevator up directly from the kitchen to cook right in my suite. "Any special dietary restrictions, Mr. Garrett?" This was incredible. I called my mom from the room and told her all about it. She wanted me to describe everything. The next day we started making the rounds. I appeared on *Top of Pops* to sing "Surfin' USA," along with an appearance on *Multi-Coloured Swap Shop*, a Saturday-morning live kids' TV show on the BBC, and incredibly, the young girls there were as enthusiastic as the ones back home in America. There really was something happening. *The Scotti brothers must know what they're doing*, I thought. They had marketing muscle. They were making this happen for me. And not only that, but I could fly first class and stay in the best places in the world. This all seemed too good to be true.

Bad Habits

Traveling from country to country, England to Spain to Germany and beyond, I slowly started to notice how much I was beginning to drink. Drinking underage was easy to get away with because I was always with the adults. They always treated me as an equal, and the booze was always free-flowing, so I took part. And then I had a gold American Express card in my own name, so there was never an issue. Nobody ever told me not to have another one; rather, they upped the ante with drugs, pulling me aside and asking, "Hey, kid, want to do a line?" I guess none of the adults in charge had any kids because, if they did, I doubt they would've allowed this to happen to their fifteen-year-olds. This was a very critical moment in my life. I was often lonely and missing my friends and family back home. There was nobody else for me to hang out with on the road besides my manager and, usually, a couple of promo guys from the hosting country. Drinking became a way for me to deal with the boredom and blur of constant travel and endless promotional appearances.

Those trips were hardly vacations, though I did try to have fun. I remember skateboarding on the streets in Germany and putting on a real show for the locals, who seemed to love watching a classic Southern California kid do his thing on a board. But those moments were few and far between. Sometimes, I was in my room alone and I got depressed, sitting in these massive hotel rooms throughout all of these countries. Sometimes I'd cry. I missed home. I couldn't always leave the hotel without security, so those gorgeous rooms became like prison cells.

But plenty of other times, I would bring women back to my suite. The routine set in: sex, room service, listen to music, watch TV. Repeat.

The cycle of being on the road and having to go out and do what everybody wanted me to created an unhealthy set of habits. It's another one of the reasons I think I began self-medicating. I wasn't happy about my existence, and I certainly wasn't happy about the songs that I was being forced to lip-synch on all those TV shows. I would hear them playing the record, and while all of the girls swooned, I would think, *That's barely me singing. That's really Jim Haas. That's whose voice you love.* And, of course, that would lead me to drink even more after the performance because I knew I wasn't being real with anyone. I wanted to numb my existence, so I did. And in the absence of any real responsible adult or chaperone, I was free to do what I wanted. Think about it. If you were traveling through Europe with your fifteen-year-old son or daughter, how would you feel if he or she was drinking, taking Quaaludes, and snorting cocaine continually? I bet you would have a problem with that. That's why today, looking back, I have a problem with the way I was handled by management. Again, I definitely partook in all of these things, and nobody held a gun to my head. But I wish there had been somebody to steer me away from those things rather than just feeding me.

I got more and more frustrated. Editors at *Tiger Beat* would ask me what I was looking for in a girl. I would say something like, "I don't know; she has to be pretty, kind of like a tomboy, and very athletic." And from there they would go create these crazy scenarios about what I loved. It was all so orchestrated. They would interview me and have me make a list about things just to give them some direction, and then it was off to the races. The whole thing felt kind of wrong to me. I knew they were baiting these girls and teasing them with these questionnaires and these contests. Of course they couldn't tell the young readers what I was really like, that it was all alcohol, drugs, and sex. That would not have played well on the pages of *Tiger Beat*. But did they have to make me so squeaky clean? I was not the boy next door. I wasn't a bad kid, but I was a normal teenager who happened to be taking advantage of some pretty incredible surroundings. I was trying to get taken seriously, yet all that would happen at *Tiger Beat* was, "What's your favorite food? What's your favorite color?" Over and over and over again. It seemed very manipulative. It started making me a little bit cynical. It was hard enough being a kid, but *Tiger Beat* and other magazines were titillating these girls with fantasies that had to be confusing on some level. They were convincing these girls that this was the real me and giving these girls reason to believe that I perhaps could be theirs one day. I know it was all part of the game. But when I did appearances and I saw all the young girls with love in their eyes, part of me felt bad. I wasn't what they thought I was. Yet I acted like I was. I didn't want to let them down because they were there for me. It was such a struggle. I wasn't the first teen idol to go through this, nor will I be the last. No wonder I was drinking as much as I was. Inside, I was miserable. My acting career was growing smaller in the rearview mirror of my life. And I was starting to miss it. I was having a lot of fun being a teen idol and traveling, but inside I knew it wasn't the real me. At least with acting it's not supposed to be the real you. You understand that you're out there to play a part. But there were millions of girls all over the world who thought they knew the real Leif Garrett. And they didn't. Shit, I barely knew the guy anymore.

I always found it hard to sleep in a bed while I was on the road. My mind could not shut down. I was always overstimulated. During those craziest jet-set chapters of my life, I'd conditioned my body to grab rest wherever I could find it, and that usually meant when I was in between places. Stretched across the back seat of a blacked-out limo, with the cool and gentle hum of the motor. Lying on the floor in a jet at thirty-five thousand feet, safe in my silver metal cocoon. Nothing lulled me to sleep like those vibrations. My sleeping habits were shaped and sculpted by those rare private moments when I could squeeze into some exclusive little space, wedged in and protected from all of the sharks, vultures, and vampires. An hour here, an hour there. It didn't matter. That is where my restless soul found respite. And my body became rewired as a result. I conditioned myself to rest my body. And then invariably my manager or some other handler would shake me out of my sleep and say, "Come on, time to wake up, kid. We are landing in London." Or Madrid. Or Tokyo. Or Perth. Or any of dozens of other places around the world. Tour after tour after tour. It was a relentless blur. I would shake the sleep out of my head, run my hands through my hair a couple of times, splash some water on my face, and get ready to meet the crazy masses. Even today, lying in my bed at home, alone, I feel vulnerable. Like something could still get at me. But put me in the back of a plane or snugly fitted into a gentle rocking berth on a train, and I will find my dreams. As I learned, moving targets not only are harder to hit when enveloped by metal and separated by miles of air, they are also more at peace.

First Time in Japan: August 1978

My first trip to Japan (there would soon be several more) in the summer of 1978 was the beginning of my deep love affair with the country, its culture, and the people. Over the years, whenever I went back to Japan, I was never made to feel more welcome or respected. Part of it was the culture, and part of it was that they simply seemed to like me. Even though the audiences were naturally more sedate and in many cases not even allowed to get up and dance, I could still feel the affection from the Japanese crowds. They looked at me so longingly that I understood our special bond.

My first time over there, I was accompanied by one of my managers. He was a good guy, but like everybody else on my team, a lot older than I was. I was always the only teenager in the room. But that didn't stop us from visiting a place in Kawasaki, in the greater Tokyo area, our very first stop in Japan, that he had been raving about on the plane ride over. He wanted to hit one of the legendary, classic Japanese massage parlors. I remember it very vividly. We walked into this huge, well-lit place that had stadium-style seating, featuring rows and rows of Japanese women who sat doing their nails and watching TV with bored expressions. I wasn't quite sure what the deal was, but my manager set me straight right away. "Pick a girl, Leif. Pick any girl you want. You're going to love this." I was still just sixteen years old, and even though I had started having sex with a fair number of women, this was a unique experience. The guy who seemed to run the place came out, snapped his fingers, and all the girls stopped what they were doing and stood up in a line, waiting for us to choose. There was something very mechanical and robotic about it, but I did what I was told. I pointed at a beautiful girl with green eyes and short brown hair, who led me down to a small private room with a white tile massage table. Next, she sat me on a small stool, and then proceeded to wash me from head to toe. She cleaned every inch of me. Then she lay me on the table and said under her breath, "Breast massage." It was actually quite remarkable, and I liked it. This was not what most sixteen-year-old boys were experiencing in terms of sex. Most guys my age were probably in the back seat of their Plymouth Duster trying to awkwardly undo the bra of their prom date. Me? I was being tended to by a high-priced Japanese masseuse who was gorgeous to boot. After my breast massage, she did the most amazing thing. Somehow—and I still can't figure out how—she ran her mouth down around me and put a rubber on me that she had hidden in her mouth. I almost couldn't believe it. At no time did I have any idea she had it in there. But she did it perfectly. Then we had sex—very methodical and deliberate, but also very good. There was a caring quality to her as she looked deep into my eyes and made sure I was satisfied. As soon as we were done, she removed the rubber, washed me off, and sent me on my way. I met up with my manager outside. He was still salivating after his experience. Somewhere, another teenage boy was going to a ballgame with his dad. Here I was in Japan, exiting a massage parlor with my manager. "Oh, he connected with that one and it's out of here; a home run!"

For the next ten days, we toured the country—Tokyo, Osaka, Kyoto, and other places—before heading to Manila, in the Philippines, for more promo appearances. I wasn't performing concerts; I was merely lip-synching on television shows and showing up to sign autographs for thousands of screaming girls. The thing I remember most about being in Japan was that whatever studio I happened to be arriving at, there were hundreds of fans waiting for me, all wearing flaxen hair wigs to match my real locks. That was incredible.

Tenerife

Later in the summer of 1978, it was back to Europe for another grueling cycle of promo appearances featuring endless in-store appearances, interviews, and, of course, lip-synching in TV studios. Still no live shows with a real band.

My mom was with me on this trip, and our first stop was Spain. Specifically, we were headed for the picturesque speck in the sea called Tenerife, the largest and most populated of the Canary Islands. I liked having my mom along, as she didn't usually go on promotional trips like this. But at the last minute, a seat opened up, and so she was excited. She was with me plenty of times when I was touring around the United States; in fact, on the road, she used to trim my hair when she was with me, and more than once I remember promoters and editors offering her money for my hair. They always wanted to sell it or give it away as a promotional item in their magazines, which I thought was crazy.

Anyway, heading to Tenerife, at first I was a little bit freaked out. I was aware that just one year before, the deadliest disaster in aviation history had occurred on the island when two Boeing 747 jets collided on the runway, killing 583 people. It was a huge news story, and I was thinking about it as we touched down at the same airport where it happened. Feeling relief as we pulled up safely to the gate, Tad Dowd, another member of the Scotti Brothers team who'd been sent by the Scotti brothers to keep an eye on me for this trip, told me that the reason we were stopping at this white sand paradise was to shoot a segment for a big television variety show in Spain called *La sonrisa de un niño*. I would be lip-synching (what else?) my new single, a cover of the nearly twenty-year-old Paul Anka hit "Put Your Head on My Shoulder," which had become a huge hit in that country. Sounded simple enough. By now I had the lip-synch thing down pretty well. I hated doing it because of how fake all of it was, but by now it was part of the deal and I made the most of it.

What greeted us, though, was nothing like I expected. The main street was lined with thousands of people who evidently had been breathlessly awaiting my arrival. This was not cool. In my heart, I was still an actor. I knew how to memorize lines, turn up on set, hit my mark, and deliver my performance. At this point in my life I was still used to controlled performing environments. But this was not that. The director, a well-known Spaniard named Valerio Lazarov, described what he wanted me to do, which was basically to walk along this thoroughfare, lip-synching my song while thousands of people oohed and ahhed over me. Something came over me. I just could not do it. Maybe I was tired from the flight, or maybe I was cranky about the whole concept, but I knew that I was not comfortable around all those people. Understand, I was still basically a shy kid who was getting used to being this kind of performer. Something snapped. I had a meltdown, with my mom standing there watching. I lost it. "I'm not doing this!" Tad didn't know what to do, so he called Tony back in Los Angeles. I could hear Tony's voice angrily buzzing through the receiver. I think Stan had woken him up. He was yelling that I was to do exactly what they wanted and to "stop being such a stubborn little piece of shit."

I remember thinking, *They must have a lot wrapped up in this thing. This must be a very big deal.* But you know what? I didn't care. I just couldn't do it. It was too much pressure, but I think the real reason I was refusing to lip-synch may have been that I hated the song along with the lame concept for the performance.

The director and other parts of the production team were all getting in my face, saying in broken English, "You can't back out; look at what we've done for you! This is all for you! We have done this all for you!" That was making it worse. The pressure and guilt this all put on me made me want to yell even louder. I didn't want to hear that they had done all of that for me. I didn't want any of it.

What was supposed to have been a moment in paradise was quickly becoming a sentence in hell. I asked Tad for alcohol but was told that it was impossible, that there were some restrictions because it was Sunday.

It took me a few minutes to calm down, and then I calmly tried to assess the situation. "Okay," I told them. "We can do the performance here, but not like you have it choreographed. I want something much quieter with far less pressure on me. If you can figure that out, then we can get this done."

Everybody huddled up, and within maybe an hour or so there was an alternate plan. The crowd, much to everyone's dismay, was ordered to disperse, and then we drove up to a spot high on a hill overlooking the turquoise water in the harbor.

There was a beautiful historic landmark called The House of Balconies, and we shot up there. We traveled to quiet parts on both hillsides of the valley. The calm, serene locations helped to ease my nerves, and I gave them what they wanted. It's funny though because, if you look at that video today, you can see I do not look happy. There's no smile. I think it's the only time that ever happened to me on camera, when a dark mood took over and did that to my performance. On the drive back down, I decided to pay Tad back for this fiasco by driving like a madman along the treacherous, winding road until he got sick. I had only my learner's permit, but I was still a good, if somewhat risk-taking, driver. Both he and my mother were white-knuckling in that car, but that's how I was starting to deal with things. As obnoxious as my behavior on this day may sound, it was really just me lashing out. I wasn't comfortable being the Leif Garrett who was being sold to people. It was getting tiresome, and more and more did not fit my personality or personal tastes.

John Belushi

I loved playing soccer. In fact, around this time I was invited to play in weekend games that were quietly held at a little park on Coldwater Canyon on the Beverly Hills side, next to the fire station. Rod Stewart was part of the group that played, along with some other rock stars and world-class international soccer players. That was amazing in and of itself, and it led to a kind of friendship with Rod. I mean, at least, I'd get invited up to his parties at his house once in a while, or a dinner. Soccer was a big part of my life at this time, so it was cool to learn that Warner Communications (Atlantic Records' parent group at the time, now called Warner Music Group) owned the New York Cosmos professional soccer team, featuring the internationally famous player Pelé (interestingly, part of his Cosmos salary came from being an artist on Atlantic). Warner had a big event at the Meadowlands stadium in New Jersey, and I was thrilled to be invited. It was a fun promotion because it pulled together a lot of different artists; for me it was a blast to be hanging out with some people I admired. Rick Wakeman from the band Yes was there, along with Peter Frampton. There was a photo taken of me and Peter in which we look like twins; that became one of the more well-known images of me for that period. (I also found some time to have sex back at the hotel with one of the beautiful Cosmos cheerleaders, who, like many other gorgeous, slightly older women at this point, were simply having their way with me. And I was more than happy to oblige.)

The person I met that day whom I would actually go on to become good friends with was the comedic genius John Belushi. In June 1978, he was on top of the world. He had conquered the movies and television, and his new Blues Brothers album, *Briefcase Full of Blues*, would soon be released on Atlantic. At that point John was an absolute force of nature. He also had a ferocious appetite for drugs, and that day at the stadium, we both discovered we had more than a passing interest in Quaaludes and cocaine. We even shared a joint that he pulled out of his pocket down in the locker room before hitting the field. From that point on, whenever we were in the same city, we hung out. In fact, later in the night on the day we met, we were back in New York City in my hotel room doing blow. I loved getting to know John. He was always full of life even though he was raging out of control. He was bigger than life. And he was also another one of those guys about whom I thought, *Well, if I'm going to emulate somebody, I've probably got to take drugs just like he does.* It just seemed like the thing to do.

Joe Perry

I loved the band Aerosmith. To this day, *Toys in the Attic* and *Rocks* are two of my all-time-favorite albums. In 1978, I didn't think anybody was cooler than the "Toxic Twins," Steven Tyler and Joe Perry. They had appeared in the film *Sgt. Pepper's Lonely Hearts Club Band*, the cinematic bomb that helped, at least temporarily, to derail the careers of Peter Frampton, the Bee Gees, and a few others. It was that bad. Still, I was excited to be included in the end credits, for which they lined up dozens of celebrities and singers who were all singing the title song of the film. That was a cool day, a snapshot of who was who at the time. Here's a list of the people you can see at the end of the film:

1. George Benson
2. Jack Bruce
3. Keith Carradine
4. Carol Channing
5. Rick Derringer
6. Donovan
7. Dame Edna Everage (Barry Humphries)
8. José Feliciano

9. Leif Garrett
10. Heart (Ann and Nancy Wilson)
11. Nona Hendryx
12. Etta James
13. Dr. John
14. Nils Lofgren
15. Jackie Lomax
16. John Mayall
17. Curtis Mayfield
18. Peter Noone
19. Robert Palmer
20. Wilson Pickett
21. Bonnie Raitt
22. Helen Reddy
23. Minnie Riperton
24. Chita Rivera
25. Johnny Rivers
26. Sha Na Na
27. Del Shannon
28. Connie Stevens
29. Al Stewart
30. Tina Turner
31. Frankie Valli
32. Grover Washington Jr.
33. Hank Williams Jr.
34. Johnny Winter
35. Wolfman Jack
36. Bobby Womack
37. Gary Wright

Also, there that day on the MGM lot were George Harrison and Paul and Linda McCartney, and all three decided at the last minute to not appear on camera. When it came time for the film's premiere, I was most excited about meeting the guys in Aerosmith. Look, I was lucky. I didn't just meet a lot of my rock 'n' roll heroes; I hung out with them a lot too.

I remember being backstage at an Elton John show when his manager accosted me and accused me of unfairly criticizing the fact that Elton wasn't playing with the band that night, but rather just the percussionist, Ray Cooper. I hadn't said anything that I was being accused of, but that didn't stop the manager from getting in my face and screaming at me that I would never be welcome at another Elton John show. I mean, I was an Elton John freak. And I was getting yelled at by his manager? For something I didn't do? My life got increasingly weirder every day.

When I met the guys of Aerosmith, the last thing I wanted to come off as was a hard-core fan. I wanted to be cool, and I couldn't believe it when both Steven and Joe came over to me and started asking me questions about women they'd heard I had slept with. These guys were impressed by me? By this point, my appetite for beautiful, older women had gotten fairly strong, so I had some stories to share with the guys and I did. I couldn't believe I was standing there talking with those guys and they were actually hanging on my every word. The subject of cocaine came up, and Joe asked me if I knew where he could score. I did, and the next day there he and I were in a convertible cruising up into the Hollywood Hills to meet my dealer—who didn't believe I was actually bringing up the real Joe Perry. I think Joe and I made quite a pair, my blonde locks and his dark hair blowing in the wind as we sped up the canyon in my convertible. When we walked in, my dealer's jaw dropped. Joe and I spent the next several days getting high at the L'Ermitage hotel in Beverly Hills where Joe was staying. This was an increasing problem I was developing. I was so sick of singing all of those teen idol songs; I wanted to spread my wings and sing some real rock 'n' roll. But I also wanted to act like a rock 'n' roll star and, watching these guys, I just figured that to act like a real rock 'n' roll star meant you had to do drugs. It was part of the deal. I know that sounds stupid, but when you want to emulate somebody, you need to mimic that person's behavior, right? All of my rock 'n' roll heroes—from Keith Richards to Joe to Rod Stewart to Robert Plant to Freddie Mercury—in addition to all of them being amazing performers, all shared a fairly unhealthy love of some form of drug. Hence, if I wanted to *really* be like them and be the authentic article, then I had to do my part, and that part included lots of cocaine while I was still just sixteen years old. With zero adult supervision and, rather, a lot of adult enablers.

Skateboard

My first skateboard as a kid was a Black Knight. It was a wood board with old-school metal wheels and a jousting knight stamped on the board, and it was love at first ride. That's why getting cast in the movie *Skateboard* was a great thing for me. Getting paid to skateboard? Come on, dude. Are you kidding me? The plot line was basic: "A Hollywood agent finds himself in debt to a powerful bookie. To make a fast buck, he creates a team of exceptionally talented skateboarders and enters them in a downhill race. If they win, they will get $20,000."

It was definitely intimidating though. I was kind of the proto-typical Southern California skate rat, but I was not up to the skating abilities of a guy like Tony Alva, the "Dogtown" skateboard legend who co-starred with me in the movie. In fact, everybody who skated in the movie was a pro except me. But I think I held my own. This was around the time, and Tony was a huge part of this, when skaters began bringing their boards to empty swimming pools. That was a new thing. Shooting the movie, I would watch Tony come out of the pool's deep end totally out of the air and then drop back in over the lip of the pool. It was pretty astounding to watch. And it had an effect on me. After we finished filming throughout Los Angeles, from then on friends and I would look for empty houses that had empty swimming pools, and we would trespass and ride our boards in the pools. That was all because of what I had watched Tony doing in the film.

Tony was a total badass, and I always felt like he resented me for not being as good as the rest of the team in the movie. I mean, I had been clocked going around fifty miles an hour in a downhill, in the old-school tuck position. But what these guys were doing blew me away. Ellen O'Neal was a freestyle monster. She was doing some of the craziest and most innovative things I'd ever seen in my life.

Years later I ranted to him at a party, and he pulled me aside to apologize. "Sorry I treated you badly back then," he said, laughing. "I just didn't know what to make of you." Well, I knew what to make of him. He was and is a skateboard legend, and it was great getting to skate with the best in the world while starring in a film.

Australia

"Pop star hurt when mob of girl fans stampedes." That was the headline of the *Sydney Morning Herald* on February 26, 1978. To say that my first trip to Australia was tumultuous would be quite the understatement. I had seen some pretty intense crowds already all around the world:

"It's the same everywhere he goes...in Germany, scores of police had to be brought in to escort him to a concert date. Throughout the United States, Europe and the Orient, his visits to record stores and radio stations have resulted in riots." I was okay, though—not hurt, just shaken up a bit.

From the Far East to the Far West, I had experienced many near-riot conditions, but there was nothing like this visit to Australia. "Surfin' USA" had absolutely blown up Down Under, and from the second my plane touched down it was like Beatlemania on steroids. From Brisbane to Sydney to Adelaide, it was as if wild, stampeding teenage girls had taken over the entire country.

As soon as we arrived and got into the limousine, my manager, Stan, said to me, "This seems a lot crazier than anyplace else. We are going to need to be careful." With that, several hundred girls broke through the barricade and began shaking the limo back and forth. I thought it was going to turn over, literally. They were banging on the roof and pounding on the windows and surrounding the car entirely. The driver turned around and said to us, "Listen, you guys are paying for the damages to my car. This is ridiculous." Welcome to Australia. I could almost see a light bulb go off over Stan's head. "I think I have an idea," he told me. And so the famous armored-car routine was born. Stan decided that to get me from point A to point B, we would ditch the limo and instead hire an actual armored car: a black, heavy-duty, tank-like vehicle. Only now, it would be me and my manager inside instead of millions of dollars. I was now the most precious cargo. And the press ate that up. This was pure Scotti brothers PR magic. Stan had obviously learned well.

At my concert in the Botanic Gardens in Brisbane, many girls were injured during the stampede they created. It was total chaos. And all I was doing was lip-synching! Throughout the city, barricades were smashed down, and the whole tour played out like an extended scene from the Beatles movie *A Hard Day's Night*. It was almost comical how crazy this scene was. They actually shut down a popular city zoo at one point so I could pretty much have the whole place to myself. I'm a total animal lover, and it was fun to be able to pet and hold koala bears, kangaroos, and other local creatures. My trip coincided with the release of my movie *Skateboard*, so in addition to kids bopping to the California beach classic "Surfin' USA," skate culture, to some degree, also arrived with me, and it was fun seeing so many kids get excited about something I loved. Kids had already started skateboarding Down Under, but the movie definitely played a part in making it more popular.

My appearances were held primarily at shopping centers, and I was brought in through some hidden passageway only to step out of an elevator to be greeted by thousands of shrieking girls who were creating chaos while essentially taking over the mall. I'm not even sure how the stores could stay open. On a small stage, I lip-synched a couple of songs, and that would be it. Then it was back to the hotel, where layers of security guards were stationed throughout the lobby and whatever floor I happened to be staying on.

The newspapers down there had been running a lot of contests that gave girls a chance to meet me, so from time to time they were escorted up to my room or I would meet them down in the lobby to say hello. Most of the time they were too petrified to do little more than giggle and shake. I would try to calm them and reassure them that everything was okay, and I would thank them for their support. It was always so strange to watch reactions like this. It was one thing to be in front of thousands of shrieking girls, who almost became like one giant entity. But in the smaller meet-and-greets, I got to see the effect I was having on these young fans. And while I was flattered, it was also a little bit scary. Many of the girls would tremble uncontrollably and start crying and literally be unable to function when I met them. I would try to comfort them and keep them calm, often with no success. It just seemed like too much for them. I always reminded them that I was just another human being, and that it was scary when people grabbed and pulled at me. This was such a strange thing for me. I was the same kid I had been a couple of years ago, only I had a record out now. But this was the power of teen magazines and radio stations. Working together, they could create a bigger-than-life teen idol whom people lost control over.

At the airports, no fewer than twelve policemen or security guards would escort me from the plane into the car or through the terminal. Many of my memories during these transitional parts of the trip are simply of looking at the backs of security guys while teenage hands and arms squeezed through the ring they formed around me. They were like tentacles coming at me, grabbing at me, pulling my hair. *What if they got their hands on me? Would they hurt me? Would they rip me to pieces? Or just rip my clothes off my body and the hair off my head?* It was pure insanity.

One thing that nobody knew about my trip down there despite all the press coverage was the fact that I fell in love. Just after I arrived in Australia, in Sydney, there was a private photo shoot set up by *Tiger*

Beat magazine. They photographed me with a gorgeous local model named Anne Gillian. She was a stunning brunette, and I was smitten right away. We spent the whole day shooting the cover of this magazine together, flirting and joking, and I thought there was an obvious chemistry. We seemed comfortable enough together that I invited her to dinner that night. She arrived at my hotel suite later that evening looking even prettier than she had all day. One thing led to another, and we decided to stay in for the night rather than try to navigate what surely would have been a chaotic public date. Also, I wanted to stay in with her and get to know her better in private. She was a couple of years older than me. We drank champagne and I drew a bath for both of us. About ten floors down on the street, hundreds of girls had gathered and were chanting my name, "Leif! Leif! Leif!" all through the night.

The next morning, we both decided that she should travel with me for a couple of days because we were so into each other. I had to be careful that nobody picked up on us. This was a promotional tour to sell records and the new movie, and the press would've gone crazy had they known I'd taken up with one of their beautiful locals. After those first magical few days, she had to get back to work, and for the rest of the trip, I was miserable. I missed her terribly and thought of her all the time. By the time we arrived in Adelaide, I had repeatedly told Stan, I missed her and wanted to see her again. I liked the companionship. He told me that she was too busy working with her modeling. I was depressed. I kept going to the malls and appearing on morning show after morning show, both on the radio and on television. In Adelaide I came back from a morning appearance, walked into my suite, and there she was. Stan had found her for me, and she had gotten some time off. The rest of my trip in Australia was blissful, thanks to my time spent with Anne.

There was no way I could have had a steady girlfriend during this time in my life. It was simply too crazy, too hectic, and, quite honestly, I was enjoying having many experiences with many girls—but they usually lasted for just one night. This was a unique opportunity to spend a longer period with somebody and enjoy her company and learn about her. It would be a while before I had a real relationship, but being with Anne Gillian in Australia was as close as I got to a relationship at this time in my life.

As a postscript to this first trip Down Under, a report was released just after I returned home: "After the riots that followed rock star Leif Garrett around Australia recently, the city councils of Melbourne and Sydney are revising local laws concerning public gatherings." I guess the local officials wanted to be better prepared, as I would soon be returning there.

"Dead" Dad

When I started doing a lot of interviews in magazines and newspapers, invariably the question came up about where my father was. There was no easy answer. I never wanted to get into how difficult my early years had been or that my family had split up. It was painful, and it was also nobody's business. Before the days of the internet, when reporters couldn't easily research your family background, you could basically say anything and it would be reported as fact. I know this sounds strange, but at one point my mom suggested that I start telling reporters that my father had died. I think from her standpoint, it was kind of like a death in the family because their marriage had died. But it was also a terse answer that would end the questioning right in its tracks. So that's what I started doing. When I see the newspaper clippings today, it's very strange. I'm looking at one as I write this, an article that begins, "When he was five years old, Leif Garrett's father died, leaving his mother with almost no money and two children to raise." Or this quote from me: "When I was five, my father died. My mother, sister, and I had to adjust in a hurry. My mom had always wanted to be an actress, but her parents trained her in music instead."

Of course this was pure propaganda. It was a story concocted to both get rid of the question and perhaps even build a little sympathy. But it always felt strange for me to say this. I knew it was a lie, but it began playing into this feeling I had that much of my life was becoming concocted from lies. I wasn't really singing. My dad had died. A lot of things the teen magazines said about me weren't true. Wherever I looked, I was either being misrepresented or I was misrepresenting myself. It made me sad to tell people my dad had died. Not just because I knew it wasn't true, but because in my mind I knew our relationship was dead. So what was the difference? I never saw my father, and I wasn't sure if I would ever see him again. I was doing so many interesting and exciting things, and I would've loved to have a dad watching over me, being proud and giving me advice. Instead, I was starting to feel like the man of the house in a strange way. My mom made me feel like that too. I think a couple of times she even said that to me. "You're the man of the house now, Leif." With me starting to bring in the money that I was, I was starting to support us. Problem was, I didn't want to be the man of the house.

The Attention

The Scotti brothers had an entire formula and strategy to market me. They told me where to be and how to be; it was all about cultivating the image. They wanted me out on the town, getting my picture taken. Columns were ghostwritten in my name for all the fan magazines. Look, they were very smart. They knew they had a good thing. They were very shrewd about how they used me. Looking back, I see now that not only was I doing drugs, but for a lot of people, I had sort of *become* a drug to them. Millions of teenage girls all over the world were addicted to me.

And what about all of the teenage girls? As much as they loved me, trusted me, I loved them too. They actually believed in me. I used to joke around and say, when asked what the worst thing about being a teen idol was, "The teenage girls." When I was asked what the best thing about being a teen idol was, I would say, "The teenage girls." Knowing that there were girls who actually felt their lives were better because of me made me feel better than I have ever been able to describe. I always watched the audience closely when I was singing. I made as much eye contact as I could, and I went out of my way as much as I could to make audiences feel special. Not because I had to; because I wanted to. When I looked out at that sea of faces, it meant a lot to me. To you, the fans, I love your stories about what those concerts meant. I would never leave an arena or venue while there were still girls waiting for an autograph. I just didn't have the heart. They were doing too much for me. They may have thought I was very innocent and "the boy next door;" that's okay. That's exactly what they should have been believing back then. That innocence is something you can't replace.

I recently heard a woman talking about her experience of being a fan of mine back in the 1970s. She said she'd had a very tough upbringing, but when she walked into her room and was surrounded by all of the posters and pictures of me, it made her feel better. It was a place she could go to help her. I never realized that; the fact that mere pictures of me actually helped a lot of teenage girls cope is incredible. For everybody reading this who was out there screaming and trying to get a piece of me, trust me, you will never know what you did for me. I was struggling out there many times. It didn't look like it, but trust me, I was. I wasn't comfortable in my own skin. I was awkward. I was actually a shy teenager, as I've said, but I wasn't allowed to act that way. I knew I wasn't a real singer, but I also know that didn't bother all of you. It was more than just singing you were there for. In that respect, we needed one another, and we took care of one another.

Two press pieces from back then that were syndicated in many newspapers all over the country help recall the overall mood.

There are 160 teenage girls in the Skateway Roller Disco, all dressed to kill and brittle with excitement because their dreams are verging on reality. At any second Leif Garrett is going to walk through the door. It is almost impossible to believe. "I'm going to faint," breathes Micci Olsheski, 14. "It's just the most incredible thing." Then she looks imploringly at the reporter. "I have a picture of myself, with my address on the back. Do you think I'll get close enough to give it to him?"

—*The Ottawa Citizen*

A throng of 4000 teeny boppers gave Leif Garrett exactly this sort of hero's welcome when he visited a suburban record store recently as part of a promotional tour. Just as thunder follows lightning, a mounting swell of shrieks flooded the baby-faced pop crooner as his rabid army of followers vied for his autograph and smiles. Several fans were trampled in the fierce crunch and were taken away on stretchers. One evidently broke her leg while several others passed out. Another injured girl refused to give medics her name. "Please don't call my mother," she said, sobbing. She was clutching an autographed picture of Leif. "I cut school today and she can't find out."

—*Tallahassee Democrat*

Charity

I often wonder how different I would've been treated if I didn't look the way I did. Or let's say my face and hair were the same, but I had some serious handicap or injury. Would people have treated me the same way? Many fans seemed to lose their minds because in their view, I looked perfect. I certainly wasn't perfect. I was carrying a lot of pain and frustration around with me even though I still found a way to have a pretty good time most of the time. I always felt thankful that I had my health and that I was able to do pretty much whatever I wanted. I never thought that I looked special; that's just how I looked. That was just me. Growing up, I actually hated my looks because so many times, adults thought I was a little girl, given my hair length. So I didn't think I was anything special. But people treated me as if I were special, and I felt fortunate. That made me want to give back. I did a lot of charity work early in my teen idol career and throughout the rest of it.

I know the Scotti brothers thought it was good for public relations, and I'm sure it was, but it was important to me because it was the right thing to do. Growing up, I was always the kid who would nurse the injured bird or move the worm off the sidewalk so it wouldn't get stepped on. I always cared about anyone or anything that needed help. I'm still that way today. So when I had the opportunity to go out and be the March of Dimes spokesman, or visit hospitals and give my time to kids in wheelchairs before my shows, that was always a very serious thing for me. I took nothing for granted. If I was able to bring a smile to some kid's face who wasn't as fortunate as me, then I felt like I was doing something special. I think a lot of it goes back to a film I saw when I was little boy. It was called *Gigot*, starring Jackie Gleason. He played a deaf janitor living in a cellar in Paris. He was kindhearted, always unselfishly feeding and tending to hungry children and animals. It made a huge impression on me. As a teen idol, some of my fondest moments were getting the chance to be with kids—oftentimes my own age—who had been handed severe difficulties. For all of the craziness and debauchery, I always tried to be a good person. I did a lot of charity work (especially for the March of Dimes), and I reached out to fans as much as I could. There were many moments backstage spent with a young person who might've been disabled or at some kind of disadvantage, and it always touched my heart and reminded me how fortunate I was to be doing what I was doing. I feel the same way today with people in need.

Feel the Need and "I Was Made for Dancing"

My records sounded just like what they were: a bunch of grown men trying to repackage music they had grown up with at a time when the Sex Pistols were erupting and David Bowie, the Ramones, the Talking Heads, and other bands I loved were busy creating one of the most explosive moments in cultural history. And I was singing "Put Your Head on My Shoulder."

When I went into the studio to work on my second album—called *Feel the Need*—it was pretty much what I expected. We recorded at Michael Lloyd's place, and once again most of the tracks were complete by the time I went in to work on the songs. Michael worked hard with me, and I think he saw that I was developing somewhat as a singer. He liked that my voice was becoming "thicker" and that I could carry more parts of a tune. But I was not all there yet; I still had a long way to go. But he always told me how much he appreciated how hard I tried and what a perfectionist I was.

As predicted, these sessions were dominated by covers of long-ago hits, including "Groovin'" by the Rascals and, of course, another

Beach Boys classic, "Fun Fun Fun." There was also a pretty ballad called "When I Think of You" that had been written and recorded by Tyler James Williams. And there was something else—an original song that Michael had written—that was pretty catchy. It was definitely tailor-made for the disco nightclub craze that was currently sweeping the world in the wake of the film *Saturday Night Fever*. I didn't mind doing what to me was just a dance song. It fit the times and, again, this thing was pretty catchy.

Michael walked me through it and explained how he had come up with the melody while noodling around with an old classical piano piece he'd played as a kid. He'd played it for Tony, who liked it, and so they thought we'd give it a shot. I was up for anything at that point. I was getting sick and tired of trying to bring old songs to life, but even though it was a disco song, and even though it wasn't my first choice, at least it would break the mold of what I was doing a little bit.

The song was called "I Was Made for Dancing" and with that, I would have my biggest hit record ever. It came out in the fall of 1978 and quickly caught on. The timing was perfect. It reached number four on the UK singles chart, number ten on the Billboard Hot 100, and number two in Australia. It was big all over the world. And as quick as you can say "lip-synch," I was on a nonstop plane ride around the planet to everywhere from Japan to Thailand to London to Germany to Australia to New Zealand and beyond. It became my signature song, and even though I'm not much of a dancer, I owe a lot to Michael Lloyd for writing it. It still wasn't the music I wanted to be performing, but at least it was an original hit.

Looking back on it today, I think it's a good song. Bands I have been in recently always love to play it because it's fun to play. It's a little kitschy, but it works—it's catchy. Again, it's not what I wanted to be doing. I can't stress that enough. I wanted to be playing classic rock 'n' roll. But I have to admit, finally having a hit record that was an original song felt good.

Family and Wonder Woman

In the late summer of 1978, I taped two TV episodes that became very popular. One of them was for the hit show *Family*, which starred my friend Kristy McNichol. A lot of the teen magazines implied that we were boyfriend and girlfriend, but in reality we were just friends. The other show I did was *Wonder Woman*. What made that special was that my sister, Dawn, was also on the show. She didn't play my sister but rather a fan of the—you guessed it—teen idol that I was playing. She and I had played brother and sister before, but having her portray a semi-crazed fan was weird for me. The website Gizmodo named it one of "The 12 Most Ridiculous Episodes From the '70s *Wonder Woman* TV Series:"

> Real-life teen dream Leif Garrett plays Lane Kincaid, a fictional teen dream who gets kidnapped in the most *Wonder Woman* way possible, by a gang of chloroform-wielding dudes in ski masks. A groupie happens to see the grab, but she doesn't see the second part of the plan: the teen dream's long-lost twin brother is brought out of...wherever...to take his place, including behind the microphone at a huge concert, where he's an unexpected sensation.

Fortunately, Wonder Woman makes sure both twins survive for their awesome joint performance in matching Spandex pants. And for no reason other than it looks freaking cool, she rides in to save the day on the Wonder Motorbike, wearing the Wonder Catsuit.

Overall it was a fun episode to shoot, except for one odd moment at the start of production. I was talking to someone, and Lynda Carter wandered by and heard me say the word "fuck." (I didn't curse a lot; she just happened to catch this one.) Indignant, she stopped, turned around, and said to me, "I'd better not hear that word again out of your mouth on this set." This may have been during her born-again phase, but it still seemed a little harsh.

Ali

It seemed every day I met somebody interesting and influential. Chuck Berry. James Brown. Dick Clark. Leonard Bernstein. But I'm not sure anybody truly compared to Muhammad Ali. He was fighting Leon Spinks down in New Orleans in September of 1978, and I was going to be in the city for the entire week leading up to the event. In fact, I was going to be the grand marshal at the Parade of Champions before the fight. All in all, it was pretty crazy down there. I loved the intoxicating vibe of the Big Easy. It had an air of danger to it and a real mystique, even though I wasn't free to roam too far from where I was staying, the beautiful Royal Orleans hotel. When I traveled to events like this, I would tell someone at Atlantic Records that, if possible, I wanted to stay in hotel rooms where Jimmy Page had stayed. Anything to soak up the Zeppelin vibe. So I had Jimmy's room at the Royal Orleans.

There were so many celebrities in town for the fight, people like John Travolta and Joe Namath. I had been part of many parades already and had received countless keys to cities, but this whole thing was going to be extra special because I was going to meet "The Greatest." The New Orleans trip was kind of strange overall. The Scottis knew a cool cat named Eddie Sapir. He was very well-connected in

New Orleans—a judge in the city—and he seemed to know everybody. When we got down there, Eddie let it be known that whatever we needed, we could have. I'd met Eddie out in Vegas before this trip, at the first Ali-Spinks fight, and he seemed more connected than anyone I'd ever met. One early morning in Vegas, about four a.m., coming back from some exclusive strip club that Eddie had brought all of us to, I remember passing through a casino with him. I was too young to gamble, so as we passed the roulette table, I asked him to put ten bucks down on black twenty-two for me. He did and it hit. Everything was firing on all cylinders.

Eddie was totally dialed in with all of the politicians and cops in New Orleans. He pulled me aside at dinner one night and said, "Kid, I heard you want some company. I'll have Junior take care of it." Junior was like Eddie's "fixer" and took care of everything. And sure enough, there was a knock at my door and a beautiful woman entered. No questions asked. Stan, my manager, called me one day in my hotel room and said, "Hey, do you want to meet the champ? He's having an early-morning press conference." Meet Ali? I couldn't wait. The week had been crazy for me. There was the parade, a day was proclaimed Leif Garrett Day in New Orleans (I still have my key to the city), and I was constantly hungover. But I would not miss this. I got up early and met Ali at the press conference, which was packed. He wasn't as impressed by me as I was by him. We were photographed together, of course. A big part of the reason something like this could be arranged would be for the photographs that it would produce. Whenever I did anything having to do with any sort of public relations, Team Scotti knew that the photographs would help drive the business. I didn't care though. Any chance to meet Ali, I was up for, whether it was considered a photo op or not. After the pictures, Ali said to me, "You wanna jog with me tomorrow morning?" Evidently, he got up at the crack of dawn to jog through the streets of New Orleans. I wasn't much of a morning person, but a chance to jog with Muhammad Ali? I would never miss that.

At about five a.m. the next day, I was down in the hotel lobby, ready to go jogging, and there he was. The one and only Muhammad Ali. He had a small entourage with him, and as we left the hotel, I tried to keep up with him. We didn't say too much—I was sort of tongue-tied—but we set off to run for a few blocks in the thick New Orleans morning air. What blew my mind was that he was wearing combat boots to jog—with weights in them! It was an interesting detail to observe.

As I said, I had been in Las Vegas a few months earlier, in February, for the first Ali-Spinks bout, which was considered one of the greatest upsets in boxing history when Spinks won a split decision. Sitting in the Superdome in New Orleans on September 15, 1978, we knew we were watching something special. An estimated two billion people watched the fight worldwide in more than eighty countries. Ali won his championship back, and it was one of the most exciting events I've ever been to.

Right after the fight, it was home for a brief rest, then back to Australia for another promotional tour (which included a swing through Manila). All pretty much a total blur except for one TV appearance I did on the popular Australian TV show *Countdown*. I was lip-synching "I Was Made for Dancing," and I remember thinking, *I may not be really singing right now but still have never felt this good about a performance.* Everything clicked. I had on this amazing white suit I had purchased at Moulton's in London, one of my favorite shops (where I would also discreetly purchase cocaine with my now well-used Gold Amex card), and my white Capezio shoes and a blue striped shirt with the collar turned up. As cynical as I may have been about the lip-synching and as much of a fraud as I may have considered myself, at that moment on the show I felt like I had turned lip-synching into a true art form. Then it was time for my very first American tour. With a real band and everything! That's what I was looking forward to. That's what I was waiting for the most. This was the moment.

Mysterious Illness

Finally, at long last, a real music tour was being put together. Not some weird group of lip-synch promo stops, but an honest-to-goodness tour with a real live band. True, the band was composed of musicians who had been handpicked by the Scotti brothers and Michael Lloyd, but there were some seasoned players, and even though I think they were kind of cynical about me when they first signed on, over time we would grow close. I was excited. We began rehearsals, and it started to feel real. Originally, the Scottis wanted to hire a choreographer to come in and create moves for all of the songs, but that idea fell apart quickly. It was bad enough that I was singing what they wanted me to. I told them I wanted to move the way I wanted to move, and thankfully, they backed off. This set was going to be made up of all of my singles and then some songs that I was going to pick, like Led Zeppelin's "Good Times Bad Times." The tour covered about twenty cities, and part of the proceeds were donated to the March of Dimes. Jim Haas joined us on the road, and I had no doubt that his microphone would be much "hotter" than mine at all times. But I bit the bullet. This was still my chance to get out there and perform.

But then something weird happened. A couple of weeks before we were supposed to hit the road, my manager sat me down in the Scotti brothers' office and told me the shows were not selling out. That it was not going to look good if we went out there with any empty seats. Why weren't the tickets selling out? Had the shows not been promoted well enough? Did they need to be advertised more? I didn't know. Nobody had any answers for me when it came to those questions; the bottom line was simply, "You're not going on tour." Oh, and there was one other thing as well. My manager looked me in the eye and said, "We need to put you in the hospital." Put me in the hospital? Evidently, that was going to be the cover story. I'm not sure why. Did it keep them from losing money? Did they need to give the promoters an excuse to get them off the hook? I had no idea. But I do know that the press was informed that I had come down with a grave case of pneumonia and that I was now tucked away in a Los Angeles hospital.

So I packed a bag with enough clothes for a couple of weeks, and I went to the hospital. They had a basic room all set up for me, and it was honestly like staying in a very sterilized hotel room. Nurses stopped and asked how I was feeling, and I told them I was perfectly fine. They took my temperature and my blood pressure and listened to my lungs and heart with a stethoscope, but it was all a joke. They knew I wasn't sick, and I knew they were in on the deal. I remember thinking, *I guess if you have enough money, you can do anything.* What if somebody who was really sick needed that room? I read lots of magazines, and I did not accept any phone calls from people who had read the news that I was sick. They were simply told that I was resting and that their good thoughts would be passed along to me. It was so weird. My mom sat with me on certain days, and we looked at each other and said, "Well, I guess this is how the music business works."

The papers all over the country picked up the story. New sacks of mail arrived with letters worrying about my condition. What did I need? Was I going to live? I was 100 percent fine! It gets me angry today thinking about the fact that this whole charade of me being sick was perhaps an excuse to not have to eat the cost of canceling shows.

But that's just how it was. This is a secret I've carried around for so long, and it's a bit surreal to share it today. I was laid up in bed, and the world was told a fantastic story about how sick I was, and how tragic it was that so many fans would be disappointed to not be able to see me live and in person at last.

In the November 26, 1978 *Tampa Bay Times*, this was published:

And were it not for an attack of pneumonitis on Leif Garrett, the Bayfront would be host to four stars in five days. [The others playing the venue were Billy Joel, Donna Summer, and Ray Charles.] But tonight's Garrett date had to be broken because the 17-year-old hit maker took ill eight days ago. "He was rushed to a hospital with a fever of 104," said publicist Neil Friedman from New York. "The doctors said he has pneumonitis which is not quite as severe as pneumonia." Garrett's Suncoast debut has not been rescheduled but whirlwind box-office action before the cancellation indicates the young rocker will be welcome whenever he can make it.

I thought I hadn't been selling tickets. See why I was becoming suspicious of management?

The weirdest day was probably when David MacLeod showed up. He came by, a friend visiting a friend in the hospital (probably trying to get some alone time with me). He found it kind of weird but didn't make much of a fuss over the fact that I was okay. It's almost like he understood how show business worked. But on that same day when David was there, there was a knock at the door and my father entered. For a minute I thought I was hallucinating, but trust me, I was not doing drugs in the hospital. At least not the kind I wanted to be doing. It was really my dad. I was speechless. He came in quietly, and David looked at me. "This is my father," I said. My dad introduced himself and said that he had read about my sickness in the paper and that he wanted to stop by and see me. I had not seen him since I was a little boy—maybe ten years or so. "You've been doing pretty well for yourself," he said to me. I told him that I was staying busy, and we made some more small talk. "I saw you one day," he said. "I was working on set over at CBS, and I think you were doing your show *Three for the Road*. You were off in the distance, and there were lots of people tending to you. You were in the middle of a scene. I didn't want to bother you, but I was proud of you over there." I wish I could have responded but I was emotionally dead at that point. Numb. Here was the guy I was describing in the press as being dead. In many ways he was dead to me. Then, as quickly as he had arrived, he was gone, excusing himself and saying he didn't have a lot of time. I would not see my dad for a long time after that.

Despite the fact that the tour had been cancelled, evidently there was one show that I couldn't miss because it was too tied in to a powerful Florida radio station. So, mysteriously, I was flown to Florida to perform for four thousand crazed teenage girls.

The First Concert

Finally, it was happening. An actual concert. The first one I'd ever given. It made no sense to me why I was being "allowed" to go back and do this show near Miami, given that the world had been told I was deathly ill. It had to be another deal the Scottis had to honor. I mean, the show was being promoted by the number one radio station in Florida, Y100, and so I'm sure that had something to do with it. Either way, I was ready. I had a good band, and I was excited about finally getting a chance to be this rock star I had been pretending to be for a year. This would not be a lip-synching show. I mean, not really. But there was something semi-artificial about it. As planned, Jim Haas, the background singer who had played such a dominant part of my recording sessions, was going on the road with us. We had a sound guy who told me that while my microphone would be on, the sound level on it would be quite low. This would allow for Jim's voice to be more prominent onstage to give the songs the depth that they needed. As much as this bothered me, I understood why they were doing it this way. They wanted the show to sound good. As to why I simply couldn't take singing lessons to get where I needed to be, that was a whole other story. Nobody wanted to waste time with that. In a sense, there was no time to waste. We had to strike when we could. In my mind, I justified all of this by reminding myself that I actually would have a live microphone this time. But as our sound guy reminded me, he would be riding the level very closely so that when I spoke to the crowd or ad-libbed, he would boost it, but when it came time to sing, he would keep it low. So, on the one hand, it was kind of a sham, but it was still better than that fateful Magic Mountain appearance where I lip-synched the song three times in a row. Beggars can't be choosers. All of this said, I was still excited.

But let's not forget the fact that just days earlier, the world had been told I was quite ill.

The local papers in Florida were picking up on the weirdness of my "recovery." The *Miami News* wrote:

> Talk about a miracle cure. Teen idol Leif Garrett has been hospitalized all week in Los Angeles...but the screamy teen is back on his feet and will be appearing as scheduled tomorrow night at the Broward County Youth Fair. According to Marsa Hightower, creative services director for Scotti Brothers, Garrett's record company and management firm, "Leif will definitely be playing Miami, although the other 19 cities on the tour have been cancelled. He'll have a doctor attending him at all times, but the show is definitely on.

Why nobody in the media thought to ask why this show was okay to perform but not the others, I have no clue. Media markets were more isolated from one another then, and the world was wired differently. News simply did not travel that fast. Why other promoters didn't hit the roof, who knows? Although I'm sure there was stuff happening behind the scenes that I was unaware of. Just more unanswered questions surrounding my increasingly weird career. And no doubt it all had to do with money.

Anyway, we flew into Miami and headed over to the Gulfstream Race Track at the Broward County Fair. It was Saturday night, November 25, 1978. This was it. First time ever, live and with a real band. As I was hustled into the backstage area of the arena, I saw a bunch of young girls wearing T-shirts with my face on them, and on the back were the words, "Leif Garrett's Very First Concert!" (As I was writing this book, my coauthor and I found one of those T-shirts stowed away in a box I have at home.)

Right before showtime, the band and I got together backstage for a quick preconcert huddle. This was exciting. We could hear the crowd chanting, and when the lights came down, we heard our opening theme music, "Also sprach Zarathustra" (otherwise known as the theme from the film *2001: A Space Odyssey*), begin to play through the speakers, announcing our imminent arrival.

I was nervous, but it was different this time. This was a good kind of nervous. I was like a pent-up animal. The minute the spotlight hit me as I ran out onstage, all amped up and hyper, more than four thousand teenage girls started going wild, screaming, crying, and melting down in ways I'm sure they had never experienced before. The whole place was literally shaking. The rush of energy toward me was real. I loved having a real band behind me, and I actually did feel like a rock star. I began channeling everything I remembered from watching Rod Stewart, Mick Jagger, and Robert Plant. I preened and I posed. I pointed at certain girls and I smiled at others. The whole thing was a rush. *This is something I could get used to.* It was a relatively short set that focused on the songs that had made me famous, from "Surfin' USA" to "I Was Made for Dancing." I knew that Jim's voice was "hotter" in the mix than mine, but it was okay. The euphoric feeling of fronting a real band in front of an adoring crowd, at least for the moment, overpowered the feeling that I was a fraud. A teenage ego is weird, still wet and easy to shape. This was a cool feeling.

The reviews were okay too. As the *Fort Lauderdale News* wrote, "The voice proved clean and mellow, augmented by a smart seven-piece band." Okay, maybe it was Jim's voice they heard mostly. It didn't really matter. I was the one out front.

I mean, right?

The Astrodome

My next show was several months later, and it would take place at the world-famous Houston Astrodome. Finally, we were getting our show on the road. It was crazy from the moment we landed in Texas. Hordes of girls camped out in the hotel lobby. They were everywhere. Getting from the hotel to the famed futuristic indoor ballpark required presidential-esque maneuvering: a security detail befitting a king, including "dummy" cars and road closures.

Before we did the concerts, there had been the typical backstage "grip and grin" photo ops with local officials and contest winners. I had that stuff down pat. But not the singing in front of thousands of people.

I still wasn't a singer. Not yet, anyway. I knew my limitations. I knew how many times they layered my vocals to try to give me a "sound." And I knew who good singers were. Robert Plant. Freddie Mercury. Elton John. Those were singers. (Yet, those guys all used layered vocals, too.)

And I had never performed in any situation even remotely like this, a massive, packed stadium.

I could hear the roar of the crowd building, and I knew the lights had gone down, announcing that it was time. This was it. In my tight black spandex pants, black leather top, and Capezio dance shoes, I got up on the live white horse I'd be riding in on. They gave me my cue, and then off we went. The horse galloped into the arena, oblivious to the storm of screams, delivering me like some blond cavalry savior to the shrieking prepubescent masses. Balancing a Texas flag in one hand, I held the reins in the other and swiftly rode toward whatever fate might await me. I was smiling. Always smiling. At least as an actor I knew I could play this part. Regardless of what I felt on the inside, I'd never look scared. The house lights came up and revealed a sort of modern-day Beatlemania. The scene was chaotic; the noise was high-pitched and nearly eardrum-shattering. The band played—what else?—"The Yellow Rose of Texas" as I rode around on the horse.

I rode up to the side of the stage, dismounted, and slapped the horse on the ass so it would head back to its handler. Then I climbed the stairs, the band kicked in, and it was off to the races. My future had arrived. The sound was weird, bouncing all over the place, and the screaming threw me a bit, but after a couple of songs, I settled in. The nerves faded away, and I was actually comfortable up there. I was so happy that I had killed the Scottis' idea to have a professional choreographer give me some prearranged dance moves. They controlled enough in my life at that point, and if I was going to get up onstage in front of thousands of people, I would do it on my own terms. That was one place where they couldn't control me. So I basically cribbed from the best. A little Jagger. Some Robert Plant. A dash of Rod Stewart. A pinch of Freddie Mercury. I acted the way I thought rock stars should act. And it felt great.

The next phase of my life was now underway. Leif Garrett, the live-onstage teen idol, was now out in full force. There was no turning back.

After the show, sweaty and exhausted, I was hustled offstage—back to my airtight security detail—and whisked back to the hotel, where we went in through a secret employees' entrance to throw off my scent for the girls who had already raced back to the place for a piece of me. My tour manager and an armed security guard marched me through the kitchen, out of sight from anyone, and we took a service elevator up to my floor, which was supposed to have been locked down and secure.

As soon as we approached my room though, my tour manager abruptly stopped all of us. "Wait," he said. "Look." In the light bleeding out from under the door, we could see that there were shadows moving around. And we could hear muffled voices. My tour manager tersely ordered the guard to wait with me down the hall while he investigated. A few minutes later, he came back to us and explained, "Some girls paid the maid off to get into your room. I can't believe this happened. I caught them going through all of your stuff."

That's when I knew things had changed. As crazy as my life had become up until that point, at least I still had had some personal privacy. Sure, there were girls camped outside my house, but they could never pay anybody to get inside and go through my things. This was different. This was a violation. This was the moment I knew that my life was no longer my own, and it was scary.

Monique St. Pierre

I talked to my cousin Peter occasionally, but I hardly ever got to see him anymore, and I missed him. Once in a while he and I could escape for a quick skiing trip, but it was getting tougher and tougher to do so. I had heard stories about my family members up north—girls camping outside their houses after learning about the relation. Peter told me how the phone would mysteriously ring at all hours and they could see shadows outside in the bushes. A lot of the teenage girls up there knew I was connected to Peter and his family, so they would regularly stake out his house in the hope of catching a glimpse of me. But I was simply hardly ever there. On the phone, Peter would joke around with me and say, "The student has become the teacher." He was still my hero. He had become a world-class skier, and I loved hearing him tell me about the trips he was taking and what he was doing. But I'm not sure he could relate to my new lifestyle. A couple of times he had been down in Los Angeles and I had brought him to a few parties, and I could tell he was uncomfortable; it wasn't his world. I was now this jet-set international playboy kind of person, and I'm sure it would have been hard for most people to relate to. But Peter knew the real me. I never copped an attitude with him. Around Peter, I was still like his punk little brother. Whenever I could swing it, I wanted to bring him into my world.

I think the craziest time he and I ever had was when we went to the John Denver pro-am ski tournament in Lake Tahoe in 1979.

He and I were sharing a room, and we had a pretty fun road trip getting out there. It was sort of like old times. He was such a total stud on the slopes. He was on the covers of magazines, and everybody knew how good he was.

That night at Harrah's, in Nevada, there was a knock at the door. It was the gorgeous Monique St. Pierre, who had just been named Playmate of the Year. She was staying on our floor—with her husband, no less. Well, she and I had been checking each other out the whole time we were there, and lo and behold, there she was. Poor Peter didn't know what to do. He grabbed a blanket, crept out of the room, and went out and slept in the hallway while she and I had an amazing night.

The fun didn't end there for her and me. Peter and I were heading over to Aspen for another ski event, the Winter Nationals, a couple of days later, and Monique was going as well. Well, this time I wanted to cut Peter in on the action. There was another girl I was meeting there—one of the daughters of Ron Popeil, the famous Pocket Fisherman guy. She and Monique and I arranged with Peter to be in an amazing house that Popeil owned that had a skylight roof that looked up at the stars as the snow fell. I think it was a little too much for Peter to handle. He left the room. We did cocaine, we had champagne, and the snow fell above us. It was heavenly. The fantasy of a lifetime. Peter, you'll never know what you missed that night.

Off the Wall

One of the more confusing things about my career was how, within months of cutting a record, I was rubbing elbows with and getting to know artists who had all paid serious dues—amazing musicians I looked up to and knew I had no business being around. Rod Stewart, Elton John, Peter Frampton—I had not earned my way into this club, yet there I was. And not because of how I sounded, but because of how I looked. I never felt worthy of being around those people, but then again, I was there, and it wasn't like I wasn't going to enjoy the moments.

Growing up in the early 1970s, I loved the Jackson 5. So it was especially cool getting to know Michael and his brothers. I didn't see them that much, but there were occasionally some social settings and parties where we ran into one another—along with weird celebrity events, like the ABC-TV Rock 'n' Roll Sports Classic competition in 1978. (I'm still kind of pissed off that I came in second behind Kenny Loggins in the fifty-meter freestyle swim, but that's another story)

The Jacksons all seemed to be pretty good guys. I got to know Randy fairly well, but it was Michael who would always seek me out at these events. At that time, he and I were both appearing on the covers of many magazines and getting so much attention, we both truly related to the shared madness that had become our lives. He was always pulling me aside and asking for little pieces of advice, sort of what I imagined a kid would ask an older brother. Yet he was a couple of years older than me. It was all innocent stuff. "Hey, Leif, how do you talk to somebody you're interested in? I see you with all of those pretty girls. How do you get the nerve to talk to them? How do you get over being nervous?" Out of the entire family, it seemed like he was the only one living in a bubble. His brothers were confident and self-assured, but Michael had a shyness and soft-spoken insecurity I noticed when he and I talked privately. His lifestyle at that point was obviously the exact opposite of my endless sex and drug binges, but, of course, I totally respected his monstrous talents and also the fact that he did have an innocence about him. When traveling the world as much as all of us were at that point, I couldn't even imagine maintaining an ounce of that innocence. It was gone. Temptation was everywhere. Still, I had no idea just how innocent Michael was, or how innocent he seemed, anyway.

In February 1979, in the middle of one of my many PR swings across Europe, I traveled to the beautiful Swiss ski resort called Leysin to appear in a three-part TV spectacular. The first part was called *ABBA in Switzerland* and featured the popular Swedish singing group, along with Bryan Ferry and Kate Bush. The second part was called *Disco in the Snow* and featured Leo Sayer, Boney M., myself, the Jacksons, and others. The third part was called *Christmas in the Snow* and featured a host of other artists. They were shooting all of the episodes over four days, so the resort and all of the surrounding luxurious ski lodges were crawling with famous singers and lots of people trying to get close to the action. I was traveling alone with my road manager, Al Hassan, but I was happy when I checked into the hotel and saw the entire Jackson entourage. It was always cool bumping into people I knew throughout the world. It reminded me that we were all lucky to lead the lives we were living.

For the show, I was going to be lip-syncing my song "Feel the Need"—in the snow, no less, surrounded by five local Swiss girls posing around me and a giant snowman. The best part, though, was they wanted me to hit the slopes so they could film me skiing and incorporate it into the show. Being an avid skier, I loved the idea, but Al, on the other hand, got his ass handed to him by the Scotti brothers from back in Los Angeles when they heard about it over the phone. Their thinking was, *We can't have our little moneymaker doing something as risky as downhill slaloming in the Swiss countryside.* I felt kind of bad for Al, but there was no way I was not going skiing.

As it turned out, the Jacksons would also be filming their performance outside in the snow, lip-synching their hit "Shake Your Body." They were all wearing ski suits, and I was impressed that Michael was still hitting all of his dance moves despite the bulky outerwear. At this point in their career, even though they had just kicked off what would be a yearlong worldwide tour to support their album *Destiny*, the Jacksons were not quite as hip as they had been early in their career when they debuted as a bunch of hardworking blue-collar kids from Gary, Indiana. At this point the act was a lot more Vegas than it was Motown, but still, they worked a lot and were very popular.

One day while we were there shooting, I got bored in my hotel room and wandered down to the hotel bar. I found a few of the Jacksons, including Randy and Michael, ensconced with some of their crew members, killing time and hanging out. I joined them for small talk. I was commenting on a few girls I had my eye on, and Michael was looking at me as if he wanted to tell me something in private. We both turned our bodies away from the group at the table, and I could tell he was going to ask me for a little bit of advice, like he usually did. "Leif," he said, with a mixture of both mischievousness and excitement, "can you tell me how to...masturbate?"

Okay, I did not see this coming.

I said, "Michael, you're kidding, right?" Well, he wasn't. I could see in his eyes that he did not know how to do it and that this was a big deal for him. He was twenty years old. I didn't want to let him down, but I didn't want to go into too much detail—and I sure as hell was not going to show him. But he was my friend. "Listen, Michael,"

I whispered. "I'm going to give you my room key. Go up there and go over to my bed. You'll see a copy of *Penthouse* magazine and some Lubriderm on the nightstand. Look through the magazine and you'll be okay. If you want to take it to your room, that's totally cool. No worries." Was he blushing? I handed him the key, and he slipped away from the group.

Over a couple of Cuba Libres, I sat there wondering, *How can he not know how to masturbate? He's got all of these older brothers. Is he really that sheltered?* Apparently he was. He returned a short while later and discreetly returned my room key. I pulled him aside and said, "So? How'd it go, dude?" By now he was kind of giggling like he had done something naughty, and he told me, "I couldn't do it, Leif. I just couldn't do it. But...I looked through the magazine...Leif," he said, all wide-eyed and high-pitched. "Man, those pictures are *nasty.*"

I wouldn't see Michael again for almost a year. He and his brothers were on the road for most of 1979. But somehow in the middle of that crazy schedule he managed to squeeze in the recording of an album called *Off the Wall*. It was the game changer for him, the artistic triumph that didn't just bring him unprecedented success but also liberated him from the family act. It also changed music and would eventually influence many other big stars.

The next time I saw Michael was in January 1980 at the American Music Awards. Along with Chuck Berry, I presented Michael with the award for Favorite Soul Album of the Year, for *Off the Wall*, which would go on to sell more than thirty million copies. When he came to the podium, I felt happy for him. It was his night, but I couldn't help but flash back to that moment in Switzerland, which all of a sudden felt like a lifetime ago. "Leif...can you tell me how to masturbate?"

That kid who had been so painfully self-conscious and inexperienced was no doubt concerned as to whether he would be able to get out from under his child stardom to forge his own career, yet he had done it in the biggest of ways. He was such an enigma. On the one hand, he had asked me how to masturbate. But that same year, as was discovered recently, he wrote this letter to himself:

MJ will be my new name. No more Michael Jackson. I want a whole new character, a whole new look. I should be a totally different person. People should never think of me as the kid who sang "ABC," "I Want You Back." I should be a new incredible actor, singer, dancer that will shock the world. I will do no interviews, I will be magic, I will be a perfectionist, a researcher, a trainer, a master. I will be better than every great actor roped in one. I must have the most incredible training system. To dig and dig and dig until I find. I will study and look back on the whole world of entertainment and perfect it. Take it steps further than where the greatest left off.

It was impossible for me to have known in that hotel bar that he had it all figured out. The shy, somewhat confused twenty-year-old had a lot more going on inside than he let on, and it didn't matter if he knew how to masturbate or not. He was taking control of his future and where he was headed. Me? I had yet to even perform an actual concert at that point and barely sang on my own records. I felt like a puppet on the Scotti brothers' strings, and he was creating his own destiny on his own terms. If only I had asked *him* how to do *that*.

(You may be wondering, given what we know today about the many allegations against Michael regarding young boys, if I think he was hitting on me. Honestly, I don't know. Maybe he was. Maybe he was asking me about girls as an excuse to make a connection with me. I'll never know, and he is not here to defend himself, so I won't make any assumptions.)

The Leif Garrett Special

When I did that concert at the Astrodome, the Scottis were smart enough to film parts of it for use in an upcoming variety special on CBS. This was going to be a big deal. I was the youngest person in television history to get his own network special, and a lot was going into it. A couple of weeks after that concert, it was back over to Europe for another swing of promotional appearances through Spain, Italy, Germany, and then, finally, the UK. Most of it was a total blur, but while in London I shot an episode of *The Osmonds*, a family TV show, in which I got to perform "I Was Made for Dancing" (lip-synching at the Albert Memorial in Hyde Park with a bunch of female fans surrounding me) along with appearing in several sketches with the family. The Osmonds could not have been any further from me in terms of our social habits, but they were all nice and fairly cool, and we had a good time doing the show. It was also arranged for Marie Osmond to be one of the guest stars on my upcoming TV show, along with Brooke Shields, the comedian Flip Wilson, and a female duo musical act from Japan called Pink Lady. I had very little say in any of this; it was the Scotti brothers, along with the TV producer, Syd Vinnedge, who came up with all of these ideas.

The Leif Garrett Special

While in London, I also appeared with Bob Hope during one of his shows at the Palladium, and we also shot a comedy sketch that would be used in my show. I got to meet so many legends during this time, and he was absolutely one of the nicest. He was very funny and very sharp, and I couldn't believe that he was going to be part of my show.

I had done a lot of television around this time. When any of the networks were doing something like *Battle of the Network Stars*, *Circus of the Stars*—all of those athletic competitions or whatever—I was usually invited and I always showed up. It was very important to the Scotti brothers to have my face on television as much as it could be seen. It was a challenge getting me radio airplay because my music was not taken all that seriously, so this was a way of generating interest in me. It's why I also took part in so many key-to-the-city ceremonies and other public events: to keep my face in the papers. That was the mission. I also was a regular on many of the popular talk shows then, including *The Mike Douglas Show* and *The Dinah Shore Show*. But my show was going to be different. All of the weight of the special was squarely on my back, and it felt like a lot of pressure. These were the kinds of moments when I felt particularly embarrassed because, again, I knew inside I wasn't a singer. That was wearing me down. Even though I felt myself getting a little bit better with each record, I still knew I had a long way to go.

Recently, I was going through an old box at home and I found all of the original artwork for the show. I have to admit, it was a little unbelievable to see my picture front and center with all of the guests surrounding me. Certain aspects of my career exist in a dream state today rather than feeling as if they really happened. The network special is one of those things. It was going to be a lot of work and so, automatically, I toned down my drug intake and drinking so that I could be focused. As *People* magazine said, "Pretty babies abound as Brooke Shields and Marie Osmond join Garrett, the veteran 17-year-old actor-singer-heartthrob, in his first TV special. Bob Hope and Flip Wilson represent Leif's elders."

The beginning of the show, which was taped in Hollywood before a live audience, features clips of my early career, including a test scene from the film *Mame* with Lucille Ball—and also a clip from the infamous 1970 *Dating Game* episode that I still cringe over. Honestly, I had never seen those clips before the taping, and when they appeared on the monitor, I laughed along with the audience because they caught me so off guard. Watching myself hit those first three off-key notes of "My Best Girl" when I sang to Lucille Ball at age eight made me blush, and I think the audience enjoyed that.

The opening of the special, of course, features "I Was Made for Dancing," and there were also cuts from the show I did with Bob Hope in London, along with concert clips from the Astrodome, including one showing me riding in on the white horse carrying the flag of Texas. The network built a beautiful set for the show that included lots of blue-carpeted levels and lush pillows. One issue, however, was that the audience was seated too close to the edges of the stage. A lot of my fans were in attendance, and during one of my songs, several of them grabbed my legs and knocked me down. The show came to a complete standstill, and security guards had to come in and pull me back to my dressing room while an announcer warned everybody, "Please let the show go on without attacking the star."

Most of the show was not in front of a live audience, however. Marie Osmond had to have all of her segments completed in one day because she was due to fly back to Las Vegas to join the rest of her family for a big opening. I liked working with her. She and I did a reasonably funny sketch making fun of the song "I Was Made for Dancing" played in a bunch of different languages. The day after Marie left, it was time for my segments with Brooke Shields. She and I were going to reenact the balcony love scene from *Romeo and Juliet* during three historical periods. Even at just fourteen, Brooke was a good actress with decent comic timing. I think those segments came off well. Pink Lady, whom I had met in Japan, shot their segment in London; they were not in Los Angeles for any of the taping.

But Flip Wilson was. He was one of the funniest guys I've ever met. We did a couple of sketches together, and the one thing I learned was that if you're going to play the straight man, you have to remain totally serious. Don't go for anything funny, and stay out of the way. I especially liked when Flip was in character as Geraldine, the flamboyant woman with all of the outrageous expressions. I never imagined I would find myself on network television asking Geraldine for a date, but there I was. The special was well-received. It got decent ratings and solid reviews, and I think it showed people that I was more than just a teen idol. I mean, at least it helped remind them that I had originally started out as an actor and could still hold my own in things like comedy sketches. I think what I liked best about the special was that I could act, I could use my own voice, and I could be myself. As a singer, I had those things stripped away. But as an actor, I still felt in my comfort zone.

My Dinner With Brooke

To celebrate the success of my CBS prime-time special, Tony Scotti had a party at his house. The minute I walked into his Beverly Hills home, I couldn't help but notice that, in my opinion, it was a total reflection of his personal style: lots of tacky nouveau riche excess in red and gold—bold, loud, and gaudy.

It wasn't a big party, just the inner circle of Scotti confidants, with the addition of Brooke Shields and her mom, Teri. Brooke had been terrific on the show. Even though she was just fourteen, she wasn't just beautiful; she was funny, she had good timing, and I think the sketches she and I did were some of the highlights of the show. The mood that night was celebratory; the show had received lots of positive attention, and I think it was being viewed as a big career boost for me. But as the party was mostly adults, Brooke and I naturally gravitated toward each other. Even though she was a few years younger than I was, I still found her to be super pretty and sweet, and she seemed to have more than a little bit of a crush on me. We were talking by ourselves at one point, and I asked her, "Why don't you and I go out and have dinner one night?" I had recently gotten my driver's license, I had my new Porsche 914 2.0, and I was feeling more confident and footloose than ever as the world had begun opening for me like the oyster it was.

Her eyes lit up, and she said she'd ask her mother. Teri's reputation in the business as a hyper-protective mama bear was both well-earned and well-respected. She fiercely guarded her daughter's career, and looking back, I can honestly say, as strict as she may have come off to some, I wish my mom had done the same thing. That said, I should not have been too surprised when later in the evening, with a death-ray stare and more than a little alcohol on her warm breath, Teri whispered to me, with disarming calm, "You touch her, I'll kill you. If there are any photos taken, I'll kill you. Do you understand?" I nodded slowly, expressionless, quite confident in her promise to deliver (I will add that, for some strange reason forever lost in the mists of time, this conversation took place under a table, just the two of us).

I pulled Tony aside that night and said, "Look, I want to take Brooke out to dinner this week, but it needs to be very discreet. Teri means business. I don't want to die. I need you to help me out."

My idea was to take her to Ma Maison over on Melrose. The restaurant had been opened several years earlier, in 1973, by a Parisian named Patrick Terrail, and it was *the* place—so exclusive that its phone number was unlisted. As the saying went, "If you don't have the number, we don't want you." Well, Tony had the number, and he discreetly told me he would set up a reservation for me for a few nights later, which he did.

When I picked Brooke up for our date, she looked beguiling, and wise far beyond her mere fourteen years. We were both dressed to the nines, and I will say, we made a killer-looking couple. Teri gave me that death stare once more as I walked Brooke out the front door of their home. She didn't have to even say it. We now had a simple, unspoken understanding: I violate policy, I die.

On the ride over to the restaurant, we were both a little giddy. It was rare for us to have time like this without adults hovering all over the place, and we were going to make the most of it. But then as we approached the restaurant, we both saw it: a gaggle of maybe ten or twelve paparazzi photographers who all trained their lenses on my car just as I was about to pull up, like big-game hunters scoping out elusive, precious prey. Word of our grand arrival had obviously leaked, and I learned later, it was the Scotti brothers who had done the leaking. PR mavens that they were, it was always all about the photo op, usually at the expense of my privacy. As I imagined Teri Shields in the middle of the mob with a shotgun, Brooke freaked out. "If pictures of us get out, my mom will kill me! And then she'll kill you!" She said this with zero irony as I nodded but stayed calm. I didn't want this young damsel to be in any distress (me either!), so I came up with the quick idea. I avoided the restaurant and cut into a back street about a block away. I had been to Ma Maison, and I knew it had a back patio that butted up against a cinder block wall, maybe six feet high, that bounded someone's residential backyard. Offering the radiant Brooke my hand, we snuck quietly down the dark street and along the path adjoining the wall, avoiding all contact with anyone. "Allow me," I said to her as I helped hoist her up and over the wall before gallantly vaulting over myself, much to the shock and dismay of the exclusive patrons dining on the patio. As both jaws and forks dropped, I whisked my date through the restaurant on a beeline to the maître d' and inquired (with Bond-like savoir faire), "Garrett, party of two?"

We talked and laughed and became even better friends over dinner. Brooke was young, so I didn't have any expectations beyond enjoying her company in the seductive light of the restaurant. I was already drinking, doing drugs, having sex—I was indulging a lot by this point. So we simply talked about our lives, the increasing craziness of it all. When it came time to leave, we exited the same way we had entered, with drama and a sweep back over the wall, through the dark, and into the safe, powerful cocoon of my Porsche. Then I delivered her safely back to the protected sanctuary that was her home. It was our only date—a stolen moment, two stars in the making, streaking past each other in the night toward far different futures. But that night, we were able to be innocent teenagers living out a simple fantasy, an escape that to this day still glimmers like the fleeting fairy tale it was.

I wouldn't see Brooke again for twenty years. She was starring on a show called *Suddenly Susan,* and there was an episode built around the idea that Susan, with her thirty-third birthday approaching, realizes that there are things she hasn't done that she had written in a letter to herself that she would have accomplished by the year 2000. So she sets out to do them, and one of those things is to be kissed by Leif Garrett. The producers, noticing how torn and frayed I looked, were concerned about my drug use, but I convinced them I would be okay. I was good at that.

I never saw Brooke until we shot the episode. It was good to see her, but there was no strong connection from the past. Still, seeing her reminded me of different days. Heading out into the night, I felt hollow. I missed the 1970s, I missed being in a healthier state, and I missed innocence, even though I was never really that innocent.

Getting Out of Control

I went to Germany, Spain, England, Japan, Sweden, Switzerland, Australia—all over the world, over and over. Every television show appearance, from *American Bandstand* to *Top of the Pops*, was perpetuating my image. It all fed itself. The fan magazines covered everything, so by the time I came home, I was even bigger than when I had left. And all I had to do was go out and lip-synch whatever single happened to be hot at the time. My vocals were stacked to such a degree that it didn't even sound like a person singing. It was more like a machine, which was fitting given that that's what I was slowly becoming. A moneymaking machine. But I knew how to smile, and I had always been taught to be nice with the fans, which is actually something I'm loyal to today. I worked hard to always make a good impression when I met fans, understanding that the experience for them was something they would likely hold on to for a long time. I enjoyed that for the most part too.

I was treated sort of like an old-time classic Hollywood movie star. The more photos of me appearing out and about with pretty girls, the better it was for business. That's why I appeared at so many events. Plus, it was exciting. And I'm not sure the Scotti brothers even knew after a while what was going on when I was "out." When Studio

54 was the most exclusive club in the galaxy, I had all the access I wanted, anytime. The first time I ever walked in there (on my first promo trip to New York City), the owner, Steve Rubell, grabbed me, took me back into his office, and laid out some sparkling lines of some of the best cocaine I'd ever had. No place was too exclusive for me. One night before I headed over there, I was with a well-known actor who chopped a line out on a mirror and said, "Here you go, Leif." I thought it was coke. But it was actually my first experience snorting heroin, and I couldn't stop puking my guts out.

The next night I was back at Studio 54 with this star's wife and daughter, Liza Minnelli, Calvin Klein, Bianca Jagger, Brooke Shields, and the gorgeous model-actress Kelly LeBrock. Andy Warhol was there, too, and ended up writing about me in his published diaries. Later that same night, Kelly and I hung out together and at dawn, I raced off to the airport to catch the supersonic Concorde to London. I wished I could have spent more time with her.

This was a typical night for me in the late 1970s.

The Scotti brothers, in my opinion, cross-promoted my career at every turn, tying in records, movies, and TV whenever and however they could, squeezing every last drop of gold they could from me. Of course, I was usually oblivious to how much income I was generating, and anytime I pressed the issue, there were deflections to my questions.

This excerpt from a 1978 *People* magazine feature illustrates just how maximized the Leif Garrett brand was becoming:

> If even the hardiest of teen idols face possible fadeout when they're no longer boys, the tight-costumed Leif (rhymes with chafe) isn't worried. After all, he's had some experience in show business maturing—he has been a self-supporting pro since he was 5, was mistreated by his late father and made the columns with older women (though the reports about Michelle Phillips, 34, are false). This summer Leif caromed into his first starring movie role in Skateboard. Simultaneously his debut Leif

Garrett LP was going platinum in the wake of two gold oldies, Run-around Sue and Surfin' U.S.A. Then last month Leif gave ABC's Family a ratings boost when, in the first of two guest shots, he appeared as a teenage Lothario who confronts Kristy McNichol with her first traumatic proposition. Now Leif has come out with his second LP, Feel the Need, which he cannily hyped on an episode of Wonder Woman.

I was everywhere, but in a sense, I was also nowhere—a proverbial puppet with essentially zero control of my teenage life.

The House

I was making enough money in 1979, or at least I thought I was, that it was finally time for us to get out of the apartment in Studio City and move into a real house. As my mom had explained to me, I was basically the man of the house by now, and so I felt it was my obligation to provide for my mom and sister. But where to live? Through a real estate broker, we heard about this amazing place nestled up in the hills above Sherman Oaks. We went to visit and it was beautiful. What really impressed me about it, though, was that it was being sold by Nigel Olsson, the drummer of Elton John's band. The way the house was set up, it made sense for my mom and sister to live upstairs in the master bedroom and the adjoining bedroom. I would be living in what was essentially a basement/studio complex. It was like a cave down there, and I liked it. It was cut off from everything, and it was just what I needed back then. Nigel had set it up in a very cool way for recording, and as part of the deal when we bought the house, I kept everything in the small recording studio. This way maybe I would be inspired to eventually start making my own music, or at least be creative in a way that wasn't so controlled. I couldn't believe that I could afford a house like this now. I was still just seventeen years old. Yet

Shaun Cassidy, Andy Gibb, and I were the teen idols everybody was talking about, and I was recognized all over the world.

The other thing that was nice about the house is that it had good security. I was essentially cut off from the rest the world, and for the few months a year that I was at home, I needed that privacy and peace of mind. And, of course, the women I was seeing liked it too. My personality is such that when I do something, as the British say, it's in for a penny, in for a pound. I wanted all of everything, not just a little taste. Just as I was constantly feeding my drug and alcohol appetite, my appetite for women was probably the most intense of all. I couldn't help myself. It's just how it was. In the absence of anybody telling me to do things in moderation, I did what I felt like. The word "moderation" was never in my vocabulary. As far as being able to afford a house, all I knew was that I asked our business manager for the money and we paid the down payment. Nice and lean, easy as pie. That was just how things worked for me. Neither my mother nor I knew what questions to ask, and of course this kind of lack of knowledge would soon haunt us. But not yet. Whatever I needed, I got it. I didn't know where the money was coming from; I just knew it was there. Hey, I was traveling the world, making tons of appearances, and by now I also had hit records. I must've been making a lot of money, right? I flashed back to all of the modest apartments we'd lived in while I was growing up. This was the first real change in our lives. Our first house. I think we were all pinching ourselves. This was the next level.

Car Burial

In between all of the TV appearances, the promotional appearances and, by now, the occasional concert, I was almost never home. But when I was, I would disappear as best I could to spend time with friends and get out of the public eye. That's the part that was driving me crazy: I couldn't go anywhere anymore when I was home. If I wanted to go out to a restaurant, all kinds of arrangements needed to be made. If I wanted to sleep with a girl I met, oftentimes I would end up climbing through her window and sneaking into her bedroom while she waited there for me. Everything was undercover. But when I could get off the grid and hang out with friends privately, that's when the truly crazy things would happen. There's one incident I will never forget. I was having sex with my friend Peter's (not my cousin) girl-friend, Stephanie. He was just watching us. It was no big deal. We were at his family's two-hundred-acre compound nestled up in the Topanga Canyon forest. For several days we had been ensconced there, swimming, running around naked, doing drugs, drinking, and having lots of sex. We had created the perfect hedonistic modern Bacchanalia. There had been other girls I'd had sex with the previous nights, but then it was Peter's girlfriend. That's just how it was.

I was on top of Stephanie, and Peter reached over and nudged me. "Hey, man, it's my turn," he said, with more than a trace of awkwardness and discomfort. That's when things got weird. I woke up out of my fog. This didn't seem right. The moment totally changed, and I got off of her and said, "I just remembered I have to go home. I have something to do." Which was a total lie. I just had to get out of there.

Only I was still heavily under the influence of the drugs and alcohol. I got into my new BMW and started careening down the serpentine wooded road. I lost control, plunged into a ditch, and smacked right into a tree. This was the last thing I needed. So in my drugged-up state, I got paranoid and knew that this accident could never see the light of day. My family couldn't find out, the press couldn't find out and, most important, my insurance company couldn't find out. I staggered back up the hill and grabbed Peter and Stephanie, and they came down to help me push the car out of the ditch. There was actually a piece of the tree sticking out of the front of the car. But now what to do? The car had major damage. I had to be careful.

So in that crazy moment we concocted a scheme. We would dig a hole and bury that car right there in the woods, and no one would ever be the wiser. I would report it as stolen and that would be that. This is what narcotics do to you.

The next morning, we started digging. It was wintertime in Los Angeles, and even though it doesn't get too cold, the ground definitely gets hard. Burying the car was going to take a while, so for the next few days we would dig in the afternoon, drink and do more drugs at night, crash, and then get back at it the next day. But that hole wasn't getting deep enough fast enough. We got the bright idea to go rent an industrial drill to try to break up some of the dirt, but that became a comedy of errors. Three stoned rich kids trying to handle a heavy piece of machinery with the intent of burying an automobile in the woods. What could go wrong?

We eventually ditched the drill, did some more ludes, snorted some more blow, and smoked some more pot. And, of course, got back to digging by hand.

We also needed an alibi to report the car as missing, so we headed down to Beverly Hills for dinner at a nice restaurant. It was all part of this scheme. I waltzed into a restaurant and asked if my friends were there yet loud enough for everybody to hear that I was by myself. "No, they're not here yet, Mr. Garrett." Okay. Motive established. Well then, Peter and Stephanie walked in on cue, and we had dinner together and then left. Then I rushed back inside yelling, "Oh my god, my car has been stolen!" Nobody had any clue Peter and Stephanie had simply dropped me off and waited outside before coming in for dinner. The cops were contacted, and I reported my car as a theft. Phase two was now underway.

The next afternoon we were back with our shovels pounding the hard earth, fighting through the roots to expand the hole. Each night we covered the car with leaves and fallen branches just in case anybody trespassing on the private property thought to get nosy.

Finally, on the seventh day, it appeared we had a hole big enough to place the car in sideways. As we were about to try to push it in, we heard some noises we hadn't heard all week. Something heavy was crashing through the woods toward us, and we heard voices. The three of us each stepped behind individual trees near the car to hide and wait out whatever it was. And then we saw two people on horseback approaching the scene. We had not seen anybody back there all week, and all of a sudden there are a man and woman riding horses near the partially camouflaged car. The couple stopped. The three of us were looking at one another, holding our breath. The woman said to the man, "Oh my god, I think there's a dead body in the car!" We all looked at each other. Dead body? What?

We knew we had to get out of there. But before we left I tried to wipe my fingerprints off the car. Think about that. It was my car registered in my name. But again, that's what narcotics do. I thought that by erasing my fingerprints, I could erase all attachment to the vehicle. I was out of my mind.

We got in Peter's car, and as we drove down the mountain road, we noticed two police helicopters overhead. Shit. Then four 4x4 sheriff's vehicles sped past us as they raced up the hill, followed by two cops on horseback. That couple must have alerted the entire Malibu force.

We had to get out of Dodge.

The three of us threw some things in overnight bags and raced to the Holiday Inn right by the 405 Freeway and Sunset Boulevard.

We checked in and made an executive decision: Peter and I would run out and get alcohol. When we returned to the hotel room, something about Stephanie had changed. I had a hunch what had happened, and I was right. "I called my father," she said. Her dad was a big-time lawyer, and he did what any concerned father would do. He told her to get the hell away from us and to cease any contact whatsoever. So she told us that she was going to do that. She said to us, "You know he has to call the cops and tell them you're here. So you guys really should leave."

Peter and I found a little faceless motel on Wilshire Boulevard. We must have looked like two desperate crooks on the run because basically, that's what we were. I was normally in touch with my mom frequently, but I had not called all week. I called her and she said, oblivious to my hellishly weird previous seven days, "Where have you been?"

I told her the story and then asked her if she could call my insurance company and tell them it was all a joke—that my friends had played a prank on me, and that I had the car and everything was fine. She said, "No, I can't do that. Everything is not fine. The Malibu sheriff's department just contacted me a few minutes ago, and they have your car. They towed it down from the woods. They're talking about insurance fraud; they're talking about you lying about a car theft. What is going on?"

And I realized I had to call them myself. I hung up with my mom, called the Malibu sheriff's office, and started telling them they could keep the car—that I didn't even want my beautiful metallic silvery-blue 635CSi. I apologized profusely and kept saying, "Keep the car." I had little hope that I wouldn't be arrested shortly after this phone call. But then someone told me on the phone that as long as I autographed a couple of photos for the sheriff's daughters, they would take care of everything and I wouldn't have to worry about anything. They were big Leif Garrett fans, as it turned out.

Sometimes, that's what it was like to be a teen idol. Looking back, was I happy to have beaten that rap? Absolutely. I got the same special treatment the time I was cruising up Highway 395 to go visit Peter to do some skiing. I got pulled over for speeding and the cop recognized me; he had daughters at home whom he knew would love my autograph, so case dismissed. But you know what? As good as it felt to receive this kind of special treatment, all it did was enable me, giving me evidence to believe I was untouchable. Nobody was doing me any favors. That's the problem with celebrity sometimes; everybody thinks they are helping you out by giving you special treatment, but in reality it's just another shovelful of dirt to an early grave.

The Meeting

During the next PR campaign through Japan and Europe, I started hearing a lot of new music that had yet to reach the shores of America. In particular were tunes called *"Der Kommissar"* and "Pop Muzik." There were a lot of interesting things happening overseas in terms of pop music. Synth-heavy, moody, hypnotic pop tunes were becoming all the rage. Unlike my handlers, I was beginning to grow a bit concerned about what the next phase of my singing career was going to entail. There was so much amazing music being made in the world at this time. I loved a lot of the new-wave stuff, from the Cars and the Pretenders to Elvis Costello and Graham Parker. I wanted to be making music that actually mattered. It was a no brainer. *If no one else is going to plan my career out for me, I'll do it myself. I'll put together some ideas of songs I could cover back in America.* These were great songs that I could have had hits with. None of my handlers seemed to know anything about modern music. Nobody listened to the Sex Pistols or the Police. They were still thinking about having me cover songs like "Singin' in the Rain," which I eventually did. That was still the master plan: have me just rerecord old hit records. Once a hit, always a hit. They wouldn't let me start taking singing lessons because there was no time for that. But at least this was something that I could do to affect my career.

When I got home from yet another whirlwind trip, I was anxious to sit down and tell the Scottis my ideas. I had told my manager that I wanted to have a sit-down, and evidently word got back to the Scottis that I had a lot of big ideas. I'll admit things were becoming a little bit tense with those guys by this point. I was starting to think for myself, and I also know that my behavior was getting a little bit out of control. I was going out all the time, never missing a party, seeing tons of pretty girls, and I'm sure I was a little tough to manage. I would not blame the Scottis for being frustrated with me at this point. But I was just growing up. I was no longer a little kid who needed handlers. I would soon be eighteen years old, and I had lived a pretty fast life and felt a lot older than that. All I wanted to do was be taken seriously. Unfortunately, nobody managing me cared what I thought. The fact that I had my own ideas was not going to go over well at all.

This was a big meeting. I had been summoned, along with my mother, manager, lawyer, and several other handlers to the expensive yet tacky Sunset Strip offices of Tony Scotti. He was the guy I guess you could say was responsible for turning me into the biggest teen idol the world had ever seen. Slick, charming, and East Coast Italian, he's the guy who, a few years before, after seeing all of the fan mail I was getting from teenage girls for my acting, and all the attention the teenage fan magazines were giving me, had decided there was money to be made if I was transformed into a pop singer. Lots of money. It didn't matter that I had never really sung a note in my life. After I had a gold album with Atlantic, he formed Scotti Brothers Records, just for me. Don't get me wrong, I loved music and I still do. It will always be a driving force in my life. At the age of fifteen, as I've said, I was a huge fan of Led Zeppelin, the Rolling Stones, and especially Elton John, whose classic 1973 album *Goodbye Yellow Brick Road* had already reshaped my brain and still affects me deeply to this day.

But I was not ready to be a singer when Tony first approached me. My acting career had exploded, and that's where I thought my future was. But when a charming heavy sits you and your somewhat gullible mother down and tells you that you can be a rock star, and when no one is responsibly minding your career, well, let's just say it becomes an enticing option. I also could never have imagined the amount of pure pleasure I would experience as a teen idol. The most gorgeous women, every night. The best drugs. Exciting travel. It felt like I was the Master of the Universe, and that was all good. I loved it. In fact, I didn't want it to end, which, in part, was what led to this meeting.

When we arrived in Tony's office, the mood was tense. He sat behind his desk, simmering. Something was wrong. He and his bigger, beefier brother, Ben, who was standing off to the side, always seemed foreboding to me. Ben was kind of like his enforcer. Tony was the smart one; Ben was the tough one. A goon. "Hey, Tone! Right, Tone? Whatever you say, Tone!"

Both former football players, these no-necks both understood the art of pressure and intimidation and, truth be told, their muscle definitely helped get my career to where it was. There was no denying that. But something had to give.

The sickening silence was finally broken when Tony *slammed* his fist down on the table. Everything—pens, paperweights, even the phone—bounced up from the force. That's how the meeting started. Tony glared at me before yelling, "Listen! You are getting out of control. You're not doing what I want. What you want to do is not going to help you. Do you understand? *Do you understand?*"

This was funny. Nobody at Scotti Brothers Records had ever expressed concern when record label guys and radio guys and all sorts of other industry vampires were feeding me coke, booze, and women, or trying to get in my pants. At sixteen years old! That was all fine. I always wondered, *What if those same kinds of people were treating their own children like that? Would they have stepped in and done anything?* Probably. But I was not viewed as a child. I was a piece of meat. I was the golden goose. I was the drug everybody got hooked on, and as that drug, I was abused in more ways than I'll probably ever be aware of.

The Meeting

I knew exactly what was fueling Tony's ire. This meeting was at the exact time I had started pushing back against the kind of music that I was being forced to record. As I've mentioned, I never had any say in any part of my artistic direction as a singer with the Scotti brothers. They picked the writers, the songs, the producers, musicians—everything. That might have been fine in the beginning because I didn't know anything. But as I settled into being a singer, I started to think about what I really wanted to be. I was up onstage acting out my Mick Jagger, Robert Plant, and Freddie Mercury fantasies. But the music didn't match the presentation. The music was basically lightweight disco and 1950s cover songs that the Scotti brothers had grown up loving. My big top-ten hit at the time, "I Was Made for Dancing," was catchy enough, but I wanted to push beyond that. Touring the world as many times as I had at that point for publicity appearances, I had become aware of lots of amazing music that I thought would fit me perfectly. I was out there absorbing; they weren't. I was starting to flex my muscles, spread my wings, and Tony Scotti had called this meeting to tell me he was having none of it. He was pissed. I could see him doing a slow burn, but I held my ground.

He knew I had started expressing serious thoughts about growing as an artist and appealing to my fans, who were also growing up. I never wanted any of this to end. I was living a life that to this day, I don't think anybody can imagine. I myself had become addicted to being Leif Garrett, and I wanted to do everything I could to keep him alive and well. These guys simply wanted to keep me in the same box, and I couldn't do that anymore. So I said that. I tried to gain control of my future. And Tony called this meeting to smack me back into place.

It felt like my blond, flowing hair was being blown back by the force of his roar, like in those old Memorex audio commercials. "You're nothing, kid. I made you!" he yelled, jabbing the air with his fat index finger for effect. "You don't know what the fuck is going on, you ungrateful little prick! You've got a contract with us, and you'll do what we tell you to do, understand? I'll expose you. I'll tell people the truth about your 'singing'!" With that he held up a reel-to-reel tape of my very first demos—basically threatening to blackmail me. "I made you," he snarled. "And I can break you."

So much for my gaining any control of my life. My mother and I, looking around the room at how intimidated everyone else was, were certainly not about to speak up. That was it. I felt broken. Then I stared at the floor, head hung low, feeling used, abused, and confused.

When it was "we three
against the world"
(as Mom would say).

I just wanted to
buy a big stereo
with my per diem.
Is that so wrong?

Taking my mom and my sister for a ride in my first car.

Now it's the other way around. Haha.

My great grand-
mother, my
grandmother in
the background,
my mom, and my
second cousin,
Cam.

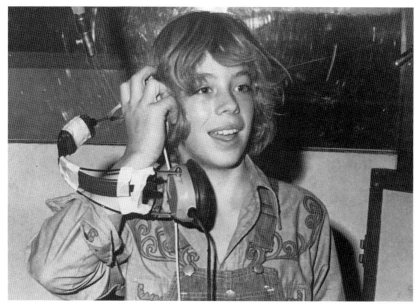

At Michael Lloyd's home studio. It looks like I've been doing this for a while, but I had no clue. At least I had the fashion down.

Nice shorts!

My first crush,
Jodie Foster.

Photo by Brad Elterman

Photo by Brad Elterman

Me hanging out with a bevy of beauties.

My sixteenth birthday with the only Scotti brother that didn't work at The Scotti Brothers.

Arriving at the first Rock 'n' Roll Olympics...and the last.

The year we all had the same hairstyle...copycats!

Showing off those smooth moves at Flippers. Check out those bitchin' roller skates with Kryptonics skateboard wheels.

My very first concert (if you can call it that) at Magic Mountain. I lip-synced "Surfin' USA" a few times.

That's right! ...With the greatest ever, Mr. Ali.

Soundcheck at the Astrodome with my bass player, Jimmy George...the whitest black man that ever lived. Nice fro, brotha!

I don't smoke them, I just light them. You're welcome, Brad and Steven.

Cops again! It just looks like I'm being arrested...I swear.

Inside the cave jacuzzi at Hef's with Kristy McNichol.

My band backstage in Japan. Bob Denoti, me, Tommy Sexton (on my left), Jim Haas (yellow shirt). That is Don Cugini hiding behind the magazine.

On our tour bus in Japan.

The sweatshirt is from the movie, *North Dallas Forty*, about football. Why the hell am I wearing boxing gloves?

On stage in Japan. By the end of the show, the streamers were up to our knees.

On tour in Japan...saying hello to fans.

In the recording studio at my home that I bought from Nigel Olsson.

On stage in Japan
in 1980.

The shot seen around the world.

I'm waiting...Nicollette and I poolside at my house.

Bet you didn't know that I'm a superhero when I'm not a teen idol.

My cousin Steven (Peter's brother) took this photo. I've always tried to be conscientious.

Apparently, Tommy Lee thinks we're in a gang.

Mom and I in New York City.

First time together in fifty-two years...Mom, me, and Dad. I don't have words!

The 1979 Tour

The summer of 1979 was going to be a big one for me. I was going to do my first American tour with a real band playing live music. Outside of the two shows I had done back in Florida and at the Astrodome, believe it or not, I still had not performed a proper tour with a band, and now I had one, which included Jimmy George, Don Cuccini, Tommy Sexton, Richard Cole, and Bobby Donati. This one was going to be grueling—basically nonstop for several months all over the country, and up into Canada as well: Six Flags Atlanta, the Mississippi State Fair, the Montana State Fair, the Indiana State Fair, the Kentucky State Fair, the Canadian National Exhibition, Six Flags Dallas, Kansas City Worlds of Fun, the Illinois State Fair, Busch Gardens Virginia, the Washington State Fair. See the theme? Lots of state fairs. The Scottis were smart when it came to this. In my opinion, they didn't want another fiasco of having to cancel the tour due to slow sales and have to put me back in the hospital. So instead they decided to book most of the shows at state fairs. It made perfect sense. State fairs had built-in audiences every day. For the price of their entrance ticket, people would get to see the show for free. That meant I would always have big crowds.

Around this time, *Parade* magazine unveiled a huge cover story featuring me and Shaun Cassidy. The headline read, "The Boy Next Door Is a Millionaire." What's interesting is that even though Shaun worked closely with Michael Lloyd, who had certainly helped shape my music, we'd never met. In fact, to this day I have never met Shaun. We were always getting pitted against each other on all of the teen magazines, almost challenging girls to take sides. But there were obviously enough teens to support both of our careers.

I was ambivalent about the tour. On the one hand, I was excited about finally being able to get out there day after day singing music in front of crowds, developing a stage persona, and even getting to cover some of my favorite tunes by Led Zeppelin and the Rolling Stones. Maybe this is how I would finally be taken seriously as a singer. But wait. Not so fast. The ubiquitous Jim Haas would also be on the road with us, no doubt with a much "hotter" microphone than mine to make sure all of the notes were in the right place. Michael Lloyd had been telling me that he thought I was becoming a better singer, but clearly I couldn't hold my own yet. But I was getting better.

Would it be obvious out there onstage that my voice was not the most prominent one? Would I look foolish? Would I be exposed as the fraud that I thought I was? That's what scared me. That's what intimidated me about going out and doing a full-scale tour. Nevertheless, we hit the road in May, and it became one of the blurriest periods of my entire teen idol experience. We would usually play two shows a day, one in the afternoon and one in the evening. Right out of the gate, I learned that the problem with that was that one show was going to be better than the other. There was no way around it. It was almost impossible to go out and deliver your best in two complete shows. It was asking too much. That said, after the first couple of shows, I didn't think the audiences were going to care that much. The audience was full of lots of screaming girls who were super excited to be in the same place I was.

There wasn't much time to screw around on this tour. We would hit a town, play the shows, hop on a plane, and get right to the next city. It wasn't like the way most bands would tour—with their own bus or anything like that. This was pretty much plane to plane and out. I could bring a girl back to my hotel room, but this tour was less about that and more about grinding it out.

I think the guys in the band were very skeptical about me too. Once again, these were seasoned players who found themselves backing a singer I'm sure they knew wasn't really a singer. But they were good sports, they were getting paid, and hey, there's nothing like being on the road with a band. At the end of the day, it's still just a bunch of guys out there having a great time, checking out pretty girls, and basically living the life. I have to say though, it bothered me that we couldn't function like a true band. I was always being hustled in and out through private entrances and exits, and oftentimes was isolated from the guys.

One aspect that kept me apart from the band at times was that I was still doing a ton of press on the road. I would get into a city and do a bunch of radio and newspaper interviews while the guys in the band had some time off to either go explore or have some fun. I was basically booked out the entire time. In terms of the crowds at the shows, I felt the love, whether it was coming from the front row or the back of the grandstand. It didn't matter. My audiences and I had our own communal thing going on, and it was positive; everybody seemed to have a good time.

The Scottis also had a pretty smart merchandising setup by then. Fans could buy key chains, wallets, programs, and so on. That was something you didn't see a lot of back then, lots of items besides just T-shirts, and I think they had great foresight in understanding that once fans were there with their parents at the state fair, there was plenty of disposable income to be had. Now, did any of that money make it back to me? I don't know. I'm not blaming the Scottis; I take responsibility for my irresponsibility and not asking the questions, but I still wonder to this day if I ever saw any of the merchandising money generated.

One thing I remember about the tour was how frustrating it was to be tucked away backstage all day at a state fair without being able to go out and enjoy what was going on. Hey, I was a teenager. I loved going on rides and eating junk food. I loved checking out pretty girls. I would've loved to go out and blend into the crowd and hang out and have some fun, but obviously that wasn't possible. Occasionally fans would climb up on top of bleachers to try to get a peek of us backstage, and when they did, we heard the screams. To kill time, I always kept a soccer ball to kick around, or we would throw a football, and I usually had a skateboard with me too. That way I could have some fun and get some exercise in, because otherwise, it was sort of like being trapped backstage in a cage. The guys in the band could wander around, but not me. It wouldn't be safe for anybody.

Something else I noticed on tour was how much work it is to go out and perform every day. That was a grind I had no experience with. It gave me a lot of respect for all of my rock 'n' roll idols. And even though most of the guys I looked up to did a lot of drinking and drugs, they still managed to go out and put on amazing shows day after day after day. I'm sure, subliminally, that gave me permission to believe that it was okay for me to still do those things too. But on the road, I kept things a little bit cleaner than before—for one reason, because I didn't have access to everything anymore, and for another, I needed to be in good shape every day. I would smoke pot and drink with the guys, but it didn't get much crazier than that. It had already been such an insane year, with the television show and the trips to Japan and throughout Europe.

I had started doing some commercials—including one for Idaho Potato Sticks that ran in Japan. I was doing ads for sneaker companies and clothing companies. And now I was spending this summer performing all over the United States. Many fans today tell me this was the one time they had a chance to see me in concert because it wound up being the only American tour I ever did during my teen idol days. If you saw me sing back then with a live band, this is when it would've happened. I love hearing memories from fans about this tour. A woman told me recently that she had thrown her shoes up onstage in, I think, Illinois. And she remembered that I was holding them up looking for who threw them because I knew she would need them to get home. She caught my eye, and I had one of my bodyguards take them to her. I so enjoyed watching the fans in the audience on this tour, and I tried to be very careful in giving them everything I had. If we were leaving one of the fairgrounds or other venues and I saw fans waiting late for a glimpse or an autograph, I would not leave until everybody had what they wanted. I would pose for thousands of photos and sign just as many autographs. The band would be waiting and my tour manager would be freaking out that we were going to miss the next plane, but I didn't care. If people had taken time out to come see me, I was going to do whatever I could to make their experience that much more special.

Recently I heard another fan's story from this tour that stuck in my mind. She was just fourteen years old when the band and I were rolling through upstate New York, near Niagara Falls. She stole her father's truck, loaded up her girlfriends, and drove to the concert and sat in the front row. Can you imagine that, being that determined at fourteen years old to make a dream come true? It's mind-blowing. But that's the kinds of things fans would do. And I loved them for it. Not that I would encourage anybody to go steal a vehicle to come see me, but in hindsight, it's pretty impressive.

As if I wasn't stretched in too many directions on tour, something else came up in the middle of that summer: I got booked for an episode of the TV show *CHiPs*, playing—what else?—a singer. This was going to result in the cancellation of several shows down in Florida, which was a reminder of what had happened when I'd been placed in the hospital back in 1978. But one simply could not miss shows that were being promoted by the all-powerful Y100 radio station; it was a problem. Marsa Hightower, the Scotti brothers' publicist, was brought in to run interference, and she issued this statement on my behalf:

I was so upset to hear that the concert was canceled, because I consider Miami my second home. I had my attorneys contact the producers of *CHiPs* and an agreement, as of today, has been made with them. They were advised that I would not be able to shoot for two days and I have secured permission from them to go ahead with the Miami concert. Love and kisses to everyone, Leif.

Although I would be appearing in Miami, I had to reschedule two other concerts that conflicted with the *CHiPs* shoot days, in St. Petersburg, Florida, and Evansville, Indiana. To make all three shows in two days, I had to fly back to Los Angeles after the Miami show, film *CHiPs* the next day until nine o'clock at night, then head back east on a private plane. The *CHiPs* shoot was a blast, as I got to drive a red Ferrari 275 GTB long nose—twelve cylinders, black leather interior—a perfect car. In one dramatic scene I was speeding along a part of the not-yet-opened 210 Freeway in Los Angeles, and the producers had to call for a second take. "Leif, slow down; the highway patrol needs to *catch* you in the scene."

Why do I have this running theme in my life with cops, real or not?

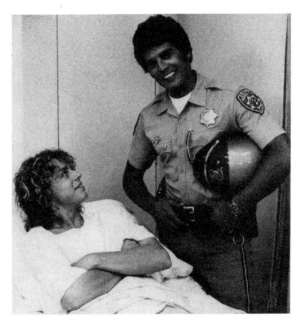

"Dear Beautiful Boy"

The 1979 tour was very successful and enjoyable, but it also had a dark side. I had some very dedicated fans for sure. There were some syndicated self-help columns in the newspapers back then, and occasionally I would see one of my fans writing to a doctor. Here's an example:

> I went to a concert to see Leif Garrett and fell in love with him instantly. I know that he could care less about me but I won't go out with any boys ever again even though I'm 16 years old. My friends think I'm crazy and my mom who is religious asked me to pray to God for guidance. Well, I did and I got this vision of Leif sending me a package with a small box in it but I checked the mail every day and it hasn't arrived yet. What do you think this vision means? Signed, Debbie from Columbus Ohio.

The good doctor answered:

> Debbie, you are living in fantasy land. Leif Garrett, I assume, doesn't know that you exist. Does he know your address? It's perfectly natural to have a crush on a "star" but keep in perspective. Give the boys in Columbus a break and start dating again. I have a vision you will meet one who catches your fancy.

The same doctor received another letter about me:

I have a most uncommon problem and I hope you can help me. Last month, my parents and I drove over 400 miles to York, Pennsylvania to see Leif Garrett in person. On the way, I bought six red roses to toss at him on stage, but we were lucky, we had front row seats. Instead of tossing the roses, Leif actually took them out of my hands, smelled them, flashed a beautiful smile and winked at me. That did it. I was hooked. A bodyguard of Leif's told me where he was staying and said if I was in the lobby by 7:30 AM, I could see him. [Gee, thanks bodyguard!] I was there the next morning and saw him in the lobby kicking a soccer ball. To make a long story short, I got his autograph, he posed for a picture and I got a kiss. That day, I was the happiest girl in the world. My three-year dream came true. My problem is that now that my dream has come true, what's left for me? I've shunned my girlfriends and dropped my boyfriend. I'm just not interested in anyone but Leif. I have over 200 pictures of him and three copies of all his albums. I feel like I care for him more than anyone else on earth, even though I hardly know him. My parents are the type who buy me anything reasonable and that's their showing of love. I simply cannot talk to them about anything. I felt love in Leif's arm when he put it around me. I saw love in his beautiful eyes. But I do realize that he's a super rock star and I'm only a fan and he probably doesn't even remember me. Please don't tell me to get rid of all the mementos that remind me of him. I just couldn't do that. I feel very mixed up I need your help. Karen

The doctor responded:

Karen, you are not unique. Girls for many generations have had crushes on movie and music stars, including Rudolph Valentino, Clark Gable, Frank Sinatra, Elvis Presley, John Travolta and yes Leif Garrett have made millions of females swoon. You were more fortunate than most. You were kissed by your idol. As you said, your three-year-old dream came true. That's good, but Karen so are other goals and dreams. You have them, they just need to be defined. So get with yourself and while you are still aglow over Leif, put these new goals in the front of your mind. Once you start fulfilling these new goals, your life will change for the better.

I couldn't make this stuff up if I tried.

I was getting fan mail from, at one point, forty-seven countries around the world. There were people who wrote me letters and sent me their scrapbooks. Other fans would go to concerts and personal appearances. There was even a group of people who used to camp outside my house.

By 1979, I could not go out in public at all without some security detail or the kind of elaborate arrangements usually reserved for heads of state. Even at home in my new house, I started to feel very claustrophobic. As I've said, there was a group of young fans who regularly camped outside, whom I would race past in my Porsche when I would come blasting out of the gates. My life became basically a series of private escapes—lots of service elevators and little-known stairwells all strategically used to get me from point A to point B. That was part of the deal. For the most part, the fans were very sweet, and I always did my best to treat them with respect. There were always a few who could get out of hand, but I tried to remind myself that I was their fantasy; for them, this was not reality. They were acting on supercharged emotions.

The only thing that scared me and the people around me was the idea that somebody could get hurt in the occasional stampede or that we ourselves might even be crushed. But then something happened that took things to an entirely new level. All of a sudden, we were all scared.

I was still getting dozens of giant sacks of fan mail delivered to the office every week. Occasionally, I would get things sent directly to my home, if the fans were clever enough to figure out where I lived.

Nobody, though, ever had access to where I stayed on the road, which is why it caught our attention when, during the summer tour, letters were waiting for me at each hotel I was staying at, left by the same person. Some of them were postmarked from Los Angeles, but others, creepily, had no postage, and so obviously had been dropped off in person. The letters all began the same way, "Dear beautiful boy..." Then this person would go on to express their deeply obsessive love for me. They would describe how they imagined us being together, going swimming, riding on motorcycles together. What was weird and even scarier was that this person seemed to know many personal details. Once the letters began referencing friends who had been swimming in my pool, with details including things like what they were wearing, we contacted the FBI. As the FBI launched an investigation, the letters continued. At hotels, I never had to check in myself; I was always whisked away while my manager took care of everything. Now I would nervously await him up in my room for news on whether or not there was a letter waiting for us. Most times, he walked in grimly holding an envelope, and I knew what it was. This was getting serious, truly a sickening distraction. I spent my time playing two shows a day at state fairs all across the country, then return to the hotel exhausted only to discover that the person had struck again. "Dear beautiful boy...I have been thinking about you all day...I love how you look in that blue bathing suit that you wore the other day with your friends at your lavish home..."

Another one read, "Beautiful boy, coming in late at night after a long drive, I said to myself, "I'm home," and I kissed your photograph as I always do... signed, Your Far Away Lover."

Then, in Ohio, my manager walked in with the envelope and said, "Look at this." That letter was different. He read it to me: "I was close enough to touch you today. But I was too scared. I wanted to. But I was too scared." On top of that, my stalker included a cartoon they had presumably drawn. It was the two of us together on a motorcycle.

As the tour cranked on through the summer, we waited for an answer, and finally it came. The FBI contacted my manager and told us there had been an arrest. They discovered that my stalker was a Los Angeles motorcycle cop who, given his job, was able to gain access to things like my home address and my itinerary. I don't recall the exact details of what happened to him, but I know restraining orders were issued and he was stripped of his badge. It was all very hush-hush, but we were told that it was finally over. I'd never been so relieved in my life. Fandom was a double-edged sword, and I accepted all of that. Most of the time, fans were wonderful. That was all good. What wasn't good—what will never be good—is when people take things too far. When the devotion and obsession morph into something dark and all-consuming. Think of all the famous people whose lives have been ruined or even lost to obsessive fans. Think of what their families have to live with then.

After that episode was resolved, they gave me the cartoon back, after it had served as evidence. I still have it today, and it remains a chilling reminder of how scary it is when somebody crosses the line. I still get a fair amount of fan mail today, which I find very touching and I appreciate. But sometimes there will be a piece that feels strange— just too much. It can still get obsessive, and I know the person writing it needs help. These moments always take me back to the summer of 1979, when I was haunted over and over by those three simple words, "Dear beautiful boy..."

Same Goes for You

Unfortunately, my next album, titled *Same Goes for You*, did little to capitalize on the success that we had with "I Was Made for Dancing." The album (which, as usual, was cut at Michael Lloyd's home studio) followed the same basic approach as my previous two albums. There were the cover tunes, including "If I Were a Carpenter" and, believe it or not, "Singin' in the Rain," which had a driving, new-wave beat that actually did sort of fit with the times. It would also become something that I enjoyed singing live, but of course there was no radio play behind it. There was another song, "Memorize Your Number," that we released as a single and that I also liked a lot. Very catchy, very jittery in that new-wave sort of style that had become popular. But that one didn't get much airplay, either. By this time the Scotti brothers had launched their own label, which didn't seem to do much in terms of making the record a big hit.

By 1979, my schedule was so crazy that I barely had any time to go in and record. When I arrived at the studio, as usual, everything was done. The record would simply be missing a "lead" vocal. But that didn't always seem to matter either. If you have a chance, listen to the song "I Was Looking for Someone to Love." Now, as I have described to you in this book, Jim Haas's voice was typically very prominent on my records. It was also very prominent onstage. But on this particular track, I don't think that's me singing at all. It sure doesn't sound like me. It sounds like Jim. Now, I'm not sure whether it ended up that way because I simply was not around to sing, or if on certain songs they just decided, *No one's going to notice; let's just make it sound as good as we can.* It does sound very good. It's a very pretty song co-written by Michael Lloyd, and I'm sure in the hands of the proper artist, it could have been hit. But I am telling you, that is not me singing. And the first time I heard it after the album came out, I was mortified. It was my worst nightmare coming true. That was not my voice on my own record. And even sadder, nobody even seemed to notice.

The Accident

Back home in Sherman Oaks after the big summer tour, I tried to settle down and catch my breath a bit. There were still a few shows I had lined up in the fall, but it wasn't a full-scale tour, just a few one-off gigs here and there. For the most part, I was home getting ready to go back to the Far East in late November. But leading up to that, I was spending a lot of time with friends and reconnecting. The tour had taken a lot out of me, and I did sort of miss the nightlife in Los Angeles.

The evening of November 3, 1979, started at Flipper's roller disco, at the corner of La Cienega and Santa Monica Boulevard in West Hollywood. In the late '70s, at the height of the roller boogie craze, Flipper's tried to be a sort of Studio 54 for those on wheels, complete with velvet ropes, VIP booths, and celebrity guest lists. While it may have lacked the mystique of Studio 54 (which I was by then well familiar with), it more than made up for it with cocaine, Quaaludes, and plenty of sexual liaisons in the private rooms upstairs. When I was home in LA, not on the road for once, many nights started there. Some ended there as well. It was a scene I enjoyed, so why not? I was at the peak of my international jet-set playboy persona, and I was treated like a god there, pretty much like wherever else I showed up.

Dope, booze, women—whatever I wanted was laid right out for me. I rarely had to lift a finger. Being a pop star, pinup, and teen idol had its perks, and I was taking full advantage of all of them. That I was totally spiraling out of control toward an almost certain early death didn't even enter the discussion.

One night, I was cruising around with a guy named Roland Winkler. I'd met him through friends a month or so earlier. He was a little older than me, twenty-one, and like many in my circle, had both time and money to burn. His family had bought him a souped-up, nitrous-fueled Mustang that he raced (and occasionally crashed) along Mulholland Drive, the infamous snake of a road that curves along the rim of the Santa Monica Mountains. I knew something about racing my black Porsche 914 along that same treacherous road, but I'd never had an accident. That night, we were hitting it hard at Flipper's. I wasn't even of legal age to drink yet (in California it's twenty-one), so Roland was buying the beer—and he also had the Quaaludes that night. Sometime near dawn, I drove us up to Kelli Campbell's house on Mulholland. She's Glen Campbell's daughter, and since her family was out of town, she was having a party at her house. Roland and I crashed there for a couple of hours, then woke up later in the morning and picked up right where we had left off. The rest of the day was spent swimming, drinking, and taking more Quaaludes. It was a typical blur. About fifteen of us, all rich and beautiful, were hanging out.

As day bled into night at the Campbell house, it became clear to everybody in attendance that we needed some cocaine to get us back up from all the booze and ludes. Our dealer, Mario, refused to come to the house, but said he would meet us instead at a little putt-putt golf place out in North Hollywood. Roland and I were chosen as the sacrificial lambs who were designated to go make the score. Fateful decision right there. Originally, Roland was going to drive his souped-up Mustang. He lived next door to the Campbells and went to get his car, but I stopped him. I knew how he drove, and I wasn't getting into a car with him. As high as I was, I still wasn't getting into a car with Roland behind the wheel. At least I had some presence of mind. So we climbed into my Porsche and headed down the hill, with me driving, into the night.

We hit the 170 Freeway toward Golfland, but thanks to our chemically altered state, we couldn't remember which exit it was. Victory? Sherman Way? We were so confused. I thought we had missed our exit, so we got off the freeway and doubled back in the other direction. It would have been the next exit, had I continued driving. I had no idea we hadn't gone far enough. I started getting agitated. Where was this place? Where was Mario? We needed blow! I'd seen the place a hundred times, and now Golfland seemed to have been wiped from the map. I looked over to my right to ask Roland about it, and he looked as if he had died. His eyes were rolled back in his head, and he wasn't answering me. He was totally unresponsive. *Little did I know that he occasionally slept with his eyes open.* With my right hand, I began jostling him to try to get a reaction. With my left hand on the wheel, I clipped the car in front of us. Then all hell broke loose.

We started to spin, and in trying to pull the car back, I overcompensated on the wheel and we ended up turned around 180 degrees, facing the traffic coming up behind us. We then hit the shoulder curb, flipped over, and began tumbling down an eighty-foot embankment. *This is it,* I thought. *We are dead.* The Targa top flew off, and the windshield caved in. But somehow, when the car finally came to rest at the bottom of the hill, I was still awake and aware. I had blood rushing out of my head from the wound I had received. But otherwise I felt intact, conscious, and suddenly, very sobered up.

After several sickening moments, Roland started saying to me, "Straighten my legs, straighten my legs!" Right there I began to suspect the worst, but I knew I had to get him help. The smell of gasoline was overwhelming, and I had no idea if the car was about to blow up. Either way, I had to get out and get help. With Roland now yelling at me, "Get me out, get me out!" I carefully climbed from the wreckage and began working my way, crab-like, up the hill. It was a cool, dewy night, and the hillside was slick and awkward to navigate. I struggled, trying to grab hold of the thick overgrowth on the steep embankment to get some traction, but I kept losing my footing. Holding on to the plants, I continued to hoist myself up, steadily pushing upward, nails digging into the moist earth, continuing my slow ascent. Two steps up, one step back. The higher I got, eerily, the more distant Roland's cries for help became.

I was aware that at the top of the embankment there were two parents and their child. The adults were yelling something down at me, and I couldn't figure it out. Once I finally reached the top of the hill, muddy, dazed, and confused, and pulled myself up, it all became clear. These were the people whose car I had clipped just before we rolled down the hill. They were furious. The father got right in my face, screaming, "What the hell do you think you're doing?" The mom was yelling at me, too, as their child of maybe six or seven watched. I knew I had hit their car, but right then and there, there was something more pressing at hand. "My friend is down there trapped in the car and he needs help," I said. "He can't move his legs and we need to get an ambulance."

They ignored what I said and kept getting in my face. I understood that I had scared them, but Jesus, couldn't they have at least tried to help us?

With the two of them droning on, yelling and cursing at me, I knew had to get away from them and call for help. I limped about thirty yards down the freeway to the roadside emergency call box. I picked up the phone and explained to the dispatcher, as calmly as I could, what had happened—that we desperately needed help. Within minutes, an ambulance, red lights flashing and sirens screaming, pulled up on the freeway shoulder and rushed down to rescue Roland. Once they reached him and eased him from the mangled Porsche, my mom arrived out of nowhere. The cops had called her, and she went with me to the hospital. While there, I saw Roland's mom and I tried to express my sorry and let her know I would help take care of him for the rest of my life. She told me that this was inevitable; that Roland had been in so many crashes already. She said it wasn't my fault.

In many ways, this was the beginning of the end for me. Just seven months earlier, I had been parading around at the Astrodome to thirty-five thousand screaming fans. I would now measure my life on either side of this tragic night. If I could mark the start of my descent into hell on a calendar, I'd scrawl a blood-red "X" on November 3, 1979.

In just five days I would turn eighteen years old.

I've never overcome the guilt and anguish from that night. That accident and its legal aftermath, coupled with my dysfunctional upbringing and stress from trying to get out from under the make-believe world the Scotti brothers had created, all worked in tandem and wound up taking their toll on me. I never knew what a house of cards my life had become, but the accident triggered a descent that would spiral for decades. Both my flesh and the fantasy that my existence had become received more than just a wake-up call that November night: It was a droning siren of death. Soon, the headlines would tell the story about this accident. It would have been much worse in the internet age, but regardless, it still got a lot of attention.

Immediately after the accident, my mom and I weren't quite sure what it all meant. I slept for literally almost three straight days after the accident without waking up, and then my mom finally roused me out of my stupor. I never wanted to wake up, but there was no escaping what had happened. We both sat there in my room, and my mom told me that someone from the office had called her. "We're going to take care of all this. Don't worry," the person told my mom. "We know how to handle this, and it's going to be okay. It's terrible what happened, but we have a good lawyer and we'll take care of everything. You don't have to worry."

This was the wire report the day after the accident:

Drunken driving charges have been filed against teen-age rock idol Leif Garrett, who was involved in a collision that destroyed his sports car and left a friend in serious condition. Garrett, 17, was arrested Saturday night after his Porsche smashed into the rear of another car on the Hollywood freeway off ramp, the California Highway Patrol said. Rowland [sic] Winkler, 19, a passenger in Garrett's car, suffered a broken neck and deep facial cuts. He was reported in serious condition at Northridge Hospital, and a spokesman said he may be permanently crippled. Garrett escaped with only a bump on the head and minor cuts. CHIP investigators said Garrett "showed symptoms" of being under the influence of alcohol. He was given a blood test at St. Joseph's Medical Center in Burbank, but the results of the tests have not been released. Garrett, who will be 18 Thursday, was released in the custody of his mother.

Two days later, this was part of the information the Scotti brothers put out to the press. Note the differences in the reporting:

Marsa Hightower, Garrett's spokeswoman with Scotti Brothers Management, said the rock star insists he hadn't been drinking. Winkler, she said, suffered an injured seventh cervical vertebra. "He is not paralyzed. There is nerve damage, but chances are he will recover."

Roland would be a paraplegic for the rest of his life.

Nicollette

In between recovering from the accident and getting ready for the tour of the Far East, I went to a pool party with a couple of friends. In the car ride over, these guys were talking about the girl who lived at the house we were headed to in the exclusive enclave of Bel Air. They said her name was Nicollette, that she was only about sixteen, and that she was absolutely beautiful. We arrived, and nothing could have prepared me for her.

I saw her on the opposite side of the swimming pool. And I swear, all the clocks stopped. Like a vision, she appeared in my view. I had to go over to her. I introduced myself, and that was it. I was lost in her. She had been born in England and now lived in Los Angeles with her mom, Sally, and her stepfather, Telly Savalas.

She simply took my breath away. It was as if I could see my future. She had long blonde hair, beguiling eyes, and the most perfect figure I had ever seen in my life. But it wasn't just about that. There was a very powerful connection that went far beyond her beauty. It's like I could see inside of her and knew she was right for me. I also loved that she didn't care who I was. That was a change. Evidently, she had a boyfriend, but I didn't care. He wasn't around, and so I stuck close by her side for the night. We ended up in the pool, just talking to each other.

Nicollette

At that point in my life, the world was my oyster and I don't think there was a woman I could not have had, anywhere in the world. But I didn't care. In that moment, I could imagine giving it all up for this girl. What was that? I had never felt anything even close to that before. I knew we were going to start seeing each other. She had such a mystique about her, and I told her I would call her as soon as I got home from the road. There was just something about her.

Back on the Road: Japan and Europe

I was still freaked out about the car accident when I went back on the road overseas. The lawyers had taken over, and some serious things were now looming over my head.

But the mood of everybody around me was like, *We have to keep moving forward; we have lots to do.* The Scottis were waiting to see what was going to happen with the lawyers, so in the meantime it made sense to get me back on the road, working and making money for everyone. Looking back on it, I should never have kept working right after that. I needed help. I should at least have been placed in rehab. It seems pretty obvious to me now that they knew my time as a teen idol was probably getting ready to wear out. The clock was ticking on how long they would be able to make money off of me. Maybe they had a year. Maybe. Had I been a veteran recording artist, they could have gotten me help and then launched a comeback. But teen idols don't get comebacks. Your moment in the sun is fleeting. Teen idols are like shooting stars; they are stunning for a moment, but then blink and they are gone. Teen idols are not like planets. They don't linger. We are there and then we are gone. In my opinion, the Scotti brothers knew exactly what they were doing. A lot of commitments had been made for me, and if I didn't show up, everybody would lose money. That was not about to happen. I guess having the Scotti brothers in control was okay on one level; I mean, at least we had somebody looking out for us. At least, that's how it seemed.

I had turned eighteen just a few days after the accident with Roland. Had it happened a few days later, my life would've been very different. I would not have been treated as a minor in the eyes of the law. Eventually, I would have my license suspended for five years. But that never stopped me from driving. At that point I felt like I was above the law. Was there any reason for me not to feel untouchable?

I had a bunch of concert tours booked later in the month, and nothing was going to stop that. I was headed to Japan and Europe and would be gone for a couple of months. I remember the management team acting like it was probably a good thing for me to get out of the country. Just go away while the whole situation died down. My life was such a blur then. There was no time to sit and think. If that accident wasn't the wake-up call that I needed help, I don't know what was. All of these adults knew that I was a functioning drug addict and alcoholic. I think my mom probably knew it too. Yet the dynamics with everybody were so screwed up that nobody thought to get me help. Even though in those days, there were not the kinds of rehab facilities you find today, I still don't think I should've been sent back out on the road. I fell right back into my habits: a different girl every night and all of the drugs and alcohol that I wanted.

Nobody in the band talked about what had happened with the accident. Really, nobody talked about it at all. It was just back to the grind. I loved being on the road and, I hate to say it, it almost made me forget about the accident. It was such another world. Back in Japan, my popularity had grown even bigger, so it was virtually impossible for me to go outside anyplace. Occasionally, there were some parties after the shows, or I could still pick out the prettiest girl and bring her back to my hotel room (but I wasn't doing it that much; I was thinking about Nicollette). And, of course, the promoters and radio guys were always there with the cocaine, ludes, or great bottles of champagne. They all knew what I had been through a few weeks before, but it didn't matter. There were no rules. The environment was so unhealthy that it's hard to imagine anybody not partaking to at least some degree, especially someone who had no strong family unit to teach him or her right from wrong.

As usual, I had a good time in the Far East, but this time I had to start disguising myself in public with a black wig. Overintense fans had begun approaching me with souvenir scissors, trying to clip locks of my now famous hair. Similar to my time in Australia, instead of using limousines I was now being transported from hotel to arena in a laundry truck to throw off the ever-present mobs. It was hectic, to say the least. But all of the touring was actually helping my singing and performing. I had a good band; I felt myself getting better. After Japan we played some dates in the Philippines, and then it was back home. Things were more serious now with the specter of a possible trial or lawsuits hanging over my head. I tried not to think about it too much, but it was tough. That night haunted me. During that time, thoughts of Nicollette helped get me through my most painful moments.

Korea

In May 1980, there was still the threat of a potential lawsuit looming over my head as a result of the accident several months earlier; yet it was announced to the public that I would become the first American contemporary music artist to embark on a concert tour of Korea. I think it was a smart move to get me over to Seoul. By now, I think the clock was ticking on how much time I had left as a teen idol—at least in the United States. It had already been a few years, which could have been considered a pretty good run by any standard. But for countries we hadn't tapped into yet, it would be a whole new experience while I was still a teenager. I would be doing ten shows in Korea after a quick European run through Spain and Italy. It was a big undertaking. We would be air-freighting ten tons of lighting and sound equipment from Los Angeles to Korea, transporting, housing, feeding, and paying a total of six performers including myself along with the crew of five people. The country was under curfew and a communist regime at that time, and from the second we touched down in Seoul, we knew we were dealing with something very different than usual.

We were transported by military escort from the airport to the hotel, and it was explained to us that the military would control the mobs of fans at the sold-out the shows. As *Billboard* magazine reported about our visit:

> The big surprise and gamble was the audience reaction, and this paid off, too. The Garrett crew said they had never seen this kind of enthusiasm, even in extroverted Australia and faddish Japan. Which meant that the teenyboppers, a new breed in Korea, were suddenly out in force. Korean girls in the 13 to 18 age bracket live in a Confucian society still dominated by males. This has been changing, they are traditionally supposed to keep quiet, stay home and behave demurely at all times. But the Garrett groupies obviously learned other lessons from imported movies, TV shows and fan articles. They were out there shrieking and stampeding with the best of them, throwing flowers and streamers onstage, not to speak of themselves, waving banners and competing with the mind-blasting sonics of a very loud show.

Martial law was interesting to observe: the helicopters and tanks patrolling all through the night. A couple of my band members even spent a night in jail for violating curfew!

The cool thing was, by this time we started to gel as a band, and I think we put on good concerts. I don't think my managers cared about that as much as they did how many tickets we sold, but I was more concerned with developing as a rock 'n' roll singer. That's now what I wanted to be. I had gotten a taste of what it was like to be up there, and I liked it. Even though I knew I was still sort of a fraud, I felt myself getting better, and that gave me hope. At the lounge atop the hotel where we were staying, my band and I would take over the bandstand and I'd get to really sing. Jim Haas never took part in those late-night jams; it was me behind the mic, and I finally started to feel as if I could hold my own. Was my management willing to work with me to help me get to the next level?

Something funny happened in Korea. Kind of. My keyboard and saxophone player's name was Richard Cole. He was a guy from Texas. Unfortunately for him, Led Zeppelin's road manager shared the same name, and so whenever we traveled, alarms always went off when they saw that name. Even though it was a different guy, it didn't matter. Poor Richard got strip-searched every which way wherever we went. After Korea, he called it quits. He couldn't take it anymore.

From Korea to Thailand to Singapore, the tour rolled on and the crowds got bigger and more enthusiastic. Even though my star was starting to fade back in the United States, in the Far East people were just catching up to me, and they loved what they saw. I still had some life left thanks to these countries.

Queen

I loved the band Queen when I was a teenager (still do). In the spring of 1980 I was flying to Munich, Germany, in first class with my manager, off to do some TV show. Seated right across from us were Andy Gibb and his manager. Andy and I were both experiencing similar realities at that point in time: We were red hot pop stars, at the apex of pinup fame. The girls loved us, and we were both experiencing success on the record charts. We made some small talk in the plush sanctuary that was first class, and once we landed in Germany, we realized we were both staying at the same hotel. The cars that were waiting for both of us pretty much drove in tandem to the hotel, and shortly after that as we were at the front desk, checking in together, I heard a loud ding announcing that an elevator had arrived. I looked across the lobby, and there they were, sauntering off the elevator and spilling out into the lobby: Brian May, John Deacon, Roger Taylor, and the flamboyant, incomprehensibly talented lead singer, Freddie Mercury. I'd met and hung out with a lot of cool people by this point, but I was still awed. This was fucking *Queen*.

They strolled past us, and then something crazy happened. Freddie Mercury cast his dark, exotic eyes upon me, gazing up and down lasciviously and practically licking his chops. Then he did the same to Andy. He was looking at both of us like we were the main course and dessert. Talk about a moment. He sashayed away and that was that. Or was it?

I finished checking in, got up to my suite and, before I even dropped my bags, noticed that the red light on the phone was blinking, indicating that I already had a message. *That's weird. I've just barely checked in. Who could be leaving me a message so quickly?*

I called down to the front desk, and the woman said to me in a thick German accent, "Mr. Freddie Mercury has just left an envelope here for you." *Well, okay then!*

I headed right back downstairs and, sure enough, there was a manila envelope for me. I opened it up and discovered a half a gram of cocaine and an invitation to go to the studio that night to watch the band record. He had left the exact same thing for Andy Gibb as well.

So, that night after dinner, Andy Gibb and I headed over to Musicland Studios, the mythical basement studio founded by the legendary Italian record producer Giorgio Moroder. Everybody from the Stones to Elton John to Zeppelin had recorded there. And it's where Queen was in the process of recording what would become the monstrously successful 1980 album *The Game* (which featured the hits "Crazy Little Thing Called Love" and "Another One Bites the Dust").

We settled in with the band, kicking back in the lounge while they took a break from recording. We did the blow that Freddie had so generously left for us, and then, incredibly, Andy and I were invited into the studio, placed behind a microphone (with Freddie!) to add some background vocals. Are you kidding me? Freddie made no more overtures toward us, but what a memory he gave us. And my experiences with Queen didn't end there. I stayed in touch with the guys, and we kind of became friends.

A few months later, they were on the road promoting the new album, and they had sold out three nights at the Forum in Los Angeles. Their drummer, Roger Taylor, rang me once the band had arrived in town and invited me to the show. I was excited. I'd never seen Queen live and had always wanted to. I arrived at the Forum and right away was taken down to the exclusive Forum Club, where a bunch of other celebrities and friends of the band were hanging out before the show, eating, drinking, and doing drugs. Roger came and found me and took me out of the room. "I want you to meet somebody," he said with an inviting grin. "Come with me."

We headed downstairs to where the band's dressing rooms were backstage, and he walked me into one of the rooms. It was empty except for a gorgeous and sexy blonde woman in a midriff crop top and hiked-up skirt, sitting by herself. "Candy," Roger said, "this is Leif. Leif, I'd like you to meet Candy." We said a little hello to each other, and then Roger added, "Candy, please take care of Leif," before leaving the room and shutting the door on his way out.

And take care of me, Candy did. That was my first real experience with a true, experienced groupie. I mean, up until that point I had been with a lot of women, but it was usually fans of mine or their mothers, along with actresses, models, or other celebrities. But this was a whole other level. Another league. This was like professional rock 'n' roll, and it blew me away (every bit of pun intended).

Rick Finch

At home, Nicollette and I were getting closer. We were still feeling out the relationship, but we knew we were dealing with something very passionate and intense. But I still was not there in terms of committing fully to her. That would happen later. In the back of my mind, I still thought she was the one, but given the amount of things thrown at me then—especially ready, willing, and available beautiful women—I wasn't quite ready to stop that yet. Then it was time to head off to record my next album, and this time it would not be done in Los Angeles with Michael Lloyd. I was going to Florida to work with someone new.

I got off the plane in Miami and made my way down to the baggage claim.

You couldn't miss him.

He looked excited to see me, with a leering ear-to-ear grin. He was in his mid-twenties, kind of scrawny, with stringy hair and a face that looked vaguely Asian...and who could forget those sweatpants, which left nothing to the imagination? My first thought was, *Dude, next time you might want to think about underwear before wearing those things again.* But hey, this was Rick Finch who had come out to pick me up, so I didn't want to judge too quickly or too harshly. This guy, the cofounder, bassist, and co-producer of KC and the Sunshine Band, had sold literally millions of records. And now, much to his seeming delight, I was in his hands.

He had recently approached the Scotti brothers to make an offer to produce my next record. I'm sure, to the Scottis, this was like manna from heaven. They could send me down to Florida for two months, which would keep me out of their hair. Yet they would know exactly where I was, so they could always keep tabs on me. But more than that, as I said, this guy knew how to make hit records. He had the goods and the pedigree, which I gathered meant he could make the Scottis money.

Ever since he was a teenager in the early '70s, working at TK Records down in Hialeah, Florida, he had made a name for himself as a skilled recording engineer, all while he was skipping high school. Then he met Harry Wayne Casey, who was working in the shipping department at the record label/recording studio. The two of them came up with a song called "Rock Your Baby" in 1974 that George McCrae recorded, and the rest was history. It became the first true disco hit, selling more than twenty million copies while helping to launch an entire new genre.

Soon after that, the two of them formed KC and the Sunshine Band (Harry Wayne Casey had become "KC"), and together they wrote and produced all of those hit records, from "Get Down Tonight" to "I'm Your Boogie Man." I was a fan. I thought those records had great grooves; they were funky in that white boy sort of way, and the hooks where undeniable. Those were killer records, and that's why I found myself, in the humid Miami spring of 1980, meeting Rick Finch.

I think I may have met him one time earlier during one of our whirlwind PR blitzes through Florida, a state where I always did good business. But nothing prepared me for the weird games of cat and mouse that were about to ensue while we "worked on my album." It started the moment he greeted me at the airport, and continued as we climbed into his souped-up muscle car. Today, looking back, I wonder if he had done his homework and learned that I was a car freak. The first thing I said as I hopped in was, "Great car, man." I was impressed, and with that, Rick floored it down the bleached Florida highway to show off the car's power, glancing over at me repeatedly as we raced toward Hollywood, a hungry glint in his eyes.

We soon arrived at his home, where, as it turned out, I stayed for two months. No hotel? Nope. This had been arranged perhaps on the one hand to save the Scottis money, but I'm guessing this also was something Rick had pushed to the Scotti brothers to agree to for his own more private, lascivious purposes.

The first thing I saw was the massive car collection, featuring mint-condition, beefed-up American muscle cars, roadsters, and more, classics one and all. It was like a museum, and my jaw must have dropped. "Wanna drive these while you're down here, Leif? All yours."

Okay, I thought. *Maybe this could work out after all.*

The property felt like something out of a Busch Gardens brochure by way of Siegfried and Roy, with a stunning aviary featuring many multicolored tropical birds. There was also a large lake, a river that ran behind the house, and lush, impeccably landscaped grounds. The moment we walked into the house, I noticed a sweet, flowery scent; it turns out it was wafting through every room. Jasmine? Gardenia? It was hard to tell, but it was everywhere. What struck me most, however, upon entering the compound (which Rick told me he shared with KC, who was nowhere to be seen) was how immaculate it was. I'm not talking just neat. His home was spotless. Modern, sharp, and angular, it was laboratory pristine. The kitchen was spick-and-span in a futuristic way, almost as if it had been air-locked in a space station. You could have eaten off the floor, had there been a visible speck of food anywhere (which there wasn't). I instantly got the impression that if I so much as nudged any one of the expensive-looking knickknacks strategically placed on several coffee tables, Rick would've instantly nudged it right back into its perfect place. Nothing was left to chance, it seemed, in this sterile environment—except maybe what he imagined happening in the bedroom.

Grandly opening the door to the room where I would be staying, as if to say, "Your suite, sir," Rick lugged my bags in for me and wasted no time in dramatically diving onto the bed, landing in a perfectly prone, suggestive pose. With one raised eyebrow he purred, "So whaddya think?"

"Umm...nice room!"

I wish someone had given me a heads-up on what to expect with Rick. I mean, someone had to have known what this guy's intentions were. Had my father been in my life at this point, I probably would have called him up and asked for a bit of advice. But as I often found during my teenage years, I was all by myself when it came to awkward situations. As with everything else, I was just going to have to figure this one out.

I unpacked my things, and then Rick asked me if I wanted to smoke some weed with him. *That's cool*, I thought. *Maybe this all isn't as weird as it seems.* Then I saw him go over to an economy-size jar filled to the top with Quaaludes. "Want one?" he cooed. "I'll have a half," I said, as once again I saw him starting to get that hungry look in his eyes. It was like the old Bugs Bunny cartoon with the guy stranded on the desert island with his friend; he starts looking at him, imagining him as a chicken on a plate. Given that I would be the chicken in this scenario, I made a mental note right there: *Do not pass out around this guy.*

Tired from the trip that day, I crashed pretty early in the evening because I knew we were going to start working the next morning. Somewhere in the middle of the night, I think about three a.m., I was awakened when, unnervingly, I felt a body curling up next to me under the covers. As Rick started spooning me, I quickly turned over and our eyes met in the dark; his, two confident slits, and mine, two large saucers like I'd seen a ghost.

"Umm, what's up, Rick?"

"Leif," he whispered. "I'm just so excited about starting work on the record. I can't sleep."

Dreaming of the nearest hotel room, I inched away ever so slightly.

"Rick, I really need some rest before we start work, you know?"

"Okay...just throwing this out there.... Care for a massage?"

"Umm, I'm good, Rick."

I could almost hear him thinking, *Curses!* Like some dastardly comic book villain whose wicked plan had been thwarted; still, he slipped calmly out of my bed, eyes locked on me as he quietly padded out of the room. I sighed deeply from relief but still squeezed my pillow from the anxiety of having to dodge this guy's advances.

For two months.

The next morning, we got into another one of Rick's incredible cars and blazed off to the studio, which was about a half an hour away. We'd be working at TK Records, the same place where all of the KC and the Sunshine Band hits had been created (along with a bunch of other well-known records). Rick kept making eyes at me on the way there. I wondered if he was thinking about some alternate plans to win me over. Whatever; I wasn't going to give it too much thought because I was pretty excited to be down there making my fourth album. For once, it was nice to not be in Los Angeles surrounded by everybody connected to the Scotti brothers. And to Rick's credit, he put together a good band in the studio, and from the moment we entered, it seemed like he had a little game plan (at least a separate game plan from trying to have sex with me). He had brought in some good cover songs to work on, including The Who's "I Can't Explain," Fleetwood Mac's "Bare Trees," and blah blah blah. His ever-present sweatpants always included full pockets of cocaine, pot and, not surprisingly, Quaaludes. In 1980, those items were almost as much of the recording process as two-inch tape and the mixing console.

I was dealing with a lot, and the recording was a nice distraction. I was still haunted by the accident, and the work helped me keep my mind occupied.

Once we all got into working and fell into a rhythm, I felt like I was more a part of the creative process than I ever had been before. One day, the band was kicking around a kind of reggae track, and I sat in and helped with the writing; it was the first time I had ever done that.

The song, "Love's So Cruel," was inspired in part by my frustration at having left Los Angeles without having consummated my relationship with my friend, Tatum O'Neal. I know that sounds weird, but it frustrated me when a woman made me wait. I had met her a couple of years earlier and had already dated two of her friends, Andrea and Carrie, who were there the night we all first got together at a Foreigner concert in LA. I liked Tatum, but it was almost like a game at that point. What would it take? So many women were throwing themselves at me, yet Tatum was keeping me waiting, and that frustration found its way into the song. At this point Nicollette was also in my life, but it hadn't become an exclusive thing yet, nor anything I was ready to start writing about in a song.

The rest of the sessions went well. It was pretty relaxed at the studio. There was always enough coke, ludes, and whatever else we needed, and outside of the few girls who might be waiting to say hi and ask for autographs outside the studio, nobody knew I was down there, so I could move about with relative freedom. On my days off, I did my best to avoid Rick's subtle advances, which, at a certain point, seemed to fade once he got the message. He got a little bitchy over that, but he still worked hard in the studio. But it was still a weird scene down there. One night when I got back to the house, I walked through the kitchen, and for the first and only time there I saw KC, his face illuminated by the light coming from the open refrigerator door. "Hey, man," I said, introducing myself, "I'm—" "I know who you are," he shot back tersely before slamming the door shut and walking out. Did he think something was happening with me and Rick?

I also connected down there with an old friend of mine, Brenda Swanson, a beautiful, athletic model I had first gotten to know on a trip to Japan. She and I had a great time together. There was a strange night that I spent with the forty-one-year-old wife of one of Rick's friends. Another friend of mine, the photographer Lynn Goldsmith, also came to the house once to shoot me posing in the pool and at the lake on the property—still some of my favorite photos of me from back then.

When I left, I did take Rick up on his offer for a bulk deal on the ludes he had; I took about 350 of them in a huge jar that I packed away in my suitcase. It was way easier back then to get away with stuff. As he dropped me off at the airport, he looked me in the eye and said, "I can't wait to see you again. I'm thinking about coming out to LA later this year." Okay, so maybe he hadn't taken the hint.

After I got back to Los Angeles, I brought the tape of the new work to the Scotti brothers' office so we could all listen to it. Tony had other ideas, though. He couldn't have cared less about the songs I played. "Here's what you are going to record tomorrow," he said gruffly, dropping a lyric sheet in front of me. "This is a song our team came up with." I couldn't believe it. I finally had a few songs cut that reflected where I was at musically. I'm not saying they were perfect, but they were a step in the right direction. But for the single, Tony was ordering me to record something called "You Had to Go and Change on Me." It was the same kind of toothless, forgettable song by committee that was now defining a singing career I had never imagined for myself. I was trying so hard to change the course of things and create music that would appeal to the audience I knew was out there. But the Scotti brothers were not about to walk away from the little girls. And this time, even they missed the boat. The single they wrote tanked. I was at least trying to connect with the audience, and I knew what was out there because I was the one on the road all the time. And their choice of this single proved they didn't have that same audience connection. All of a sudden, the end of my teen idol career started to become visible on the horizon. All around the country, music was changing. LA had a hard-core punk scene. Interesting music was pulsating in Germany, London, and other places and clubs I frequented. New-wave bands were beginning to sprout up. But you never would've known that, listening to the single the Scotti brothers made me release. I was still locked in a world where millions of little girls did nothing but worship teen magazines. But that wasn't reality anymore. Everything was changing and changing fast.

By the way, once I got back to LA from that trip to Florida, my pal John Belushi called and told me to bring over some of those Quaaludes, pronto. He was over at Universal Studios shooting *The Blues Brothers* movie. So I headed over there the next day. I knocked on the door of John's trailer, and he yelled for me to come in. The scene I witnessed was pure early-'80s excess. John, bloated and wired, was sitting at a table with a mirror that had about ten lines of blow on it. Next to that was a tray full of sushi and, next to that, a carafe of sake. He did a few lines, ate a couple of pieces of spicy tuna and yellowtail, and washed it all back with a shot of sake. Something told me he'd been repeating that cycle at that table for a long time. "Where are the Quaaludes?" he barked at me. He didn't waste a second. "Where are the Quaaludes?" "Take it easy, man," I said. "I have them right here." I took out the plastic bag full of Quaaludes I'd brought for him; he took out two and popped them in one gulp. *Three whole Rorer 714s.* A few minutes later, there was a knock on the door. The director, John Landis, needed John for his next scene, so off he went. Like it was nothing! "Wait here," he told me on the way out. So I hung out in his trailer. He returned a short while later and went right back to the mirror for more coke, then sushi and sake, like it was nothing.

Rick Finch did make it to LA later that year. He called me when he arrived and told me, "I got you an early birthday present." I met up with him, and he gave me a set of state-of-the-art Blaupunkt speakers for my car. To this day, they're the most kick-ass car speakers I've ever had. But that was as far as he got with me.

He was trying so hard to groom me and get to me, and while I was willing to accept his gifts, I certainly wasn't going to let it go any further than that. *How many other young singers has he done this with?* I wondered. This was the most destructive layer in show business, in my opinion. The preying upon beautiful young people. As I would learn later in life, my instincts had been right all along.

In March 2010, Rick Finch was arrested in Ohio, accused of having sex with a seventeen-year-old male. The local police stated that during the interview Finch gave them, he admitted to having sex with a number of teenagers from the ages of thirteen to seventeen. He eventually pled no contest to the charges and was sentenced to seven years in jail. He was fifty-six years old at the time and had been running a home recording studio where he worked with young, aspiring musicians. All seven male victims were regulars at the studio and, according to them, Finch told them that they "would need to be prepared for such activity if they sought success in the music industry."

In court, Finch blamed alcohol for his behavior. I couldn't believe he received just seven years for that. Of course, it makes me wonder what else was going on when I was down there in Florida back in 1980. I know he was trying to groom me and get me to have sex with him. But sex and drugs were viewed much differently back in 1980. Everything felt more recreational. But there is absolutely no excuse for this kind of sexual predatory behavior. I had just turned eighteen years old, so I guess technically I was of legal age. But that's not the point. I'll never know what effect that kind of pressure had on me. I'll never know how it truly affected me. I managed to escape his clutches, but how many gave in to him under the pressure, thinking that it would help their career? Did he even want to help my career back then? Or was he simply interested in sleeping with me? Once again, nobody was minding the store. There's no denying I had some fun down in Florida, and I think I did some pretty good work. But that doesn't outweigh the other issues. I don't think this man should ever have been working with young guys. I also think I was let down by my management and my family when it came to helping me deal with situations like this. In a way, this episode is the entire story of my life.

The Photo

After I got back from recording in Florida, Nicollette and I kept growing closer and closer. But I was traveling so much. Whenever I was home now, she would stay at my house. Little by little I was behaving more on the road because I knew she was back in Los Angeles waiting for me. There was another whirlwind trip to play some shows across the Far East, and right after I got back I called up Brad Elterman. He had been on the road with me over there for part of the time and, as usual, got some amazing images. But there was somebody he hadn't met yet, and I was curious what he would think of an impromptu photo shoot at my house. He'd heard about Nicollette, but he had never laid eyes on her.

The day I spoke with him, she and I had woken up early and had sex, and I thought our post-coital mood might be the perfect opportunity for Brad to try to capture some of our magic. "Come on over here now, man," I said to him. "There's somebody I want you to meet." The moment Brad arrived, I could tell he understood that Nicollette was special. As he directed us from behind the lens, he was trying not to stare too hard at her, wearing only a string bikini. Nicollette was going to change into something else, but Brad told her, "No, don't. You look perfect." I will say that on this particular morning though, we didn't need too much direction. We were both a little high, we were both feeling blissfully satisfied after our early-morning coupling, and all was right with the world.

Brad clicked away inside the house, and then he took us outside by the swimming pool. He shot a fascinating series of images of us holding each other and looking at each other. I knew right then that he was preserving the pinnacle of our romance. It was still so early in the game, and we were so madly in love with each other that little else mattered. The fights and the arguments and disagreements hadn't begun to erupt. Yet. There were no cracks in the scene yet. We intertwined as if we were one person.

After the session, Brad went over to the Scotti brothers, which is how it would often work: He would show them pictures, and they would choose the ones they wanted to distribute. The soon-to-be-famous shot on the couch was presented, and Brad told Tony, "In this one Leif has a serious hard-on." All of the girls in the office came in to gawk. That was it. That was the photo.

Those photographs, to me, represent a lot of things today. For Nicollette, I think it's the beginning. The image appeared everywhere, from *People* to *Playboy*. It put her on the map. Within a year or two she appeared in the film *The Sure Thing*. I also believe that picture captured the beginning of my end. You can see it in my eyes that the end is near. Within that same year or two, my career—at least as a teen idol—would effectively be over. Samson lost his hair and all of his power went with it; that was kind of similar for me. I was so defined by my hair. That photo today for me is like looking at the best and the worst of everything. I could not have been more in love with Nicollette, but there was no way it was going to last. She was too full of fire, and my worst habits were getting the best of me.

I met with Brad recently over coffee in Santa Monica, west of downtown LA. On his iPad we looked over hundreds of pictures he had taken of me, and a lot of memories came flooding back. But the pictures we lingered on the most were the ones he took that day at my house up in the hills. I think they are the most definitive of my life, but they were fleeting. They captured a moment that would be hard to recapture. Nicollette and I had some amazing years ahead of us, but the passion and sensuality of being teenagers in love was pure *Romeo and Juliet*. It felt like forever. It felt meant to be and meant to last. If only.

Nicollette Moves In

Things got serious when Nicollette moved into my house. But it was crazy too. For one thing, I was getting busier than ever. After my album *Can't Explain* came out, I headed back over to Europe to do shows and appearances throughout Italy and Germany. Then it was back to the US for appearances on a bunch of TV shows, including *Solid Gold*, then a beauty pageant and a bunch of other things I am hard-pressed to remember. But most important, we were too young to live together. But it felt like the right thing to do. It also raised a lot of eyebrows, given her young age of just seventeen. But we didn't care. Her mom didn't mind at all. We were in love, we were in lust, and little else mattered. Living at the house, though, created some tensions that hadn't been there before. My mom and Nicollette got along for the most part, but occasionally there were flare-ups. Two Scorpio women arguing over the Scorpio man in the house made for some interesting and intense situations. There was also tension between Nicollette and my sister, Dawn. It was awkward all the way around, but we tried to make the best of it.

The relationship, for all of its passion, was also volatile. We were both very young and reactionary. When we loved, we did so with fire, but the same went for when we argued. Everything was always a production. And yes, we were jealous of each other. If someone else so much as looked at one of us, that was cause to argue. Looking back, maybe that should have helped us appreciate each other more, the fact that others found us desirable. But we were obviously not that mature.

Nicollette and I attended the premiere of *The Sure Thing* directed by Rob Reiner in 1985. It was a big night for Nicollette. Even though her part was small, it was pivotal and people loved her. I felt like I had "discovered" her first, but the more the world got to know her, the more they fell in love the same way I did. She was that beguiling. I was planning to spend the rest of my life with her. I know that sounds crazy given my age and my circumstances, but that's how in love with her I was. I had been with so many girls up until that point, and Nicollette made me forget almost all of them. And we were so lustful! We stopped at nothing when it came to being together. It's not that our relationship was built on great sex, but it certainly was enhanced with our lack of inhibitions. I remember getting off the ski lift at Squaw Valley by Lake Tahoe; we skied down a small slope, went behind some trees, and had sex there. When I took Nicollette to London and we saw Duran Duran, even though we were backstage, we climbed up to the catwalk at the Hammersmith Odeon and had sex looking down right on top of the band. Another time I had rented a house in Lake Tahoe for New Year's, and we drove up early in the morning with my mom and sister in the back seat. While they were sleeping, Nicollette climbed on top of me as I was driving and we had sex. We were insatiable and it was unbelievable. Anytime. Anywhere. Anything went.

Brian Johnson

I forget how it all came together, but a group of us musicians who loved playing soccer were recruited to form a team that was booked to go over to Italy to play against one of the country's national teams. I was excited to be included. I want to say it had something to do with Atlantic Records because the Average White Band and Brian Johnson of AC/DC were along for the ride. So was the actor Maxwell Caulfield (who beat me out for a part in the film *Grease 2*). And the band Ace, which had that great song "How Long," also formed part of the team. Rod Stewart practiced with us in Los Angeles before we all headed over to Italy.

We were staying in a large Gothic monastery. One night I sat up late with Brian Johnson, AC/DC's then new lead singer, drinking and doing cocaine. I was a huge AC/DC fan, so it was fun hanging out with him. As we got deeper into the night, we got deeper into various subjects. "What's on your mind?" he asked me. I explained to him my general malaise about not being taken seriously as a singer or being allowed to grow as a singer. I wanted to improve. I was willing to pay my dues but nobody let me. Being around a real singer like him made me self-conscious, and I explained my whole dilemma to him. "I have no control whatsoever over my musical career," I confessed. "It's all smoke and mirrors and it's killing me. It's not how I want to be." He listened to me seriously and told me I needed to figure things out quickly. "You need to grab the reins and take control. It's your life."

By the way, we beat the Italian national team, 1–0.

Long Shot

Coming to the big screen in 1981: "Leif Garrett as a young foosball player who wants to earn the big dollars that will be used to play soccer in Europe by winning the foosball world championships."

What could go wrong?

One thing I know for certain now, and that I had a hunch about back in the early 1980s, is that teen idols seem to have a life span of no more than five years. And that's the best case. Teen idols, by design, are not meant to last, simply because kids grow up and tastes change. It's a very in-the-moment kind of thing. They fit the zeitgeist. They reflect the tastes, styles, and desires of the moment. But there is certainly no job security in being a teen idol. I knew that I needed to evolve creatively or I would probably lose my mind along with everything else. I also understood, however, that even if I was thinking this, it would make no difference if I wasn't surrounded by others who believed in that same principle. If I didn't have a like-minded team, the equivalent of what guidance counselors were advising for millions of kids my own age at the same time in college, it would be very hard for me to map out any sort of future.

When I learned that I would be starring in a film called *Long Shot*, I knew right away that I shouldn't go wasting any money on a new Oscar-night tuxedo.

It was a movie about, if you can believe it, foosball. I know. Not air hockey. Or Space Invaders. Fucking foosball. That was my next big move. It was a total embarrassment. I had been in the movie *Skateboard*, which, say what you want, was much more in tune with a national trend—skateboarding. But a movie about foosball. I still can't believe it.

I was starting to get spooked. My life was changing. The glamour, the mystique, and all of the exotic worlds I had been at the center of were either disappearing or moving on. I couldn't even tell the difference. All I knew was, I was increasingly not part of them anymore. The whole culture of teen idols had started to change. With MTV getting started and boy bands like New Edition entering the market, it was a new world. The whole *concept* of teen idols was changing. Now they could come in groups and sell four or five times what one me or one Shaun Cassidy or one Andy Gibb might be able to sell. Things were changing so fast, and there was no plan for me. When most kids my age were graduating from college, I was graduating from being a teen idol. There was no diploma; there were no companies coming to recruit me. It was a sickening feeling that life as I knew it was about to change—and not in a great way. I still had Nicollette, but even that was starting to feel threatened. Her career was beginning to take off at the same time it felt like mine was going into a free fall. That was a strange feeling. My fans were graduating to the next phase of their lives, but I wasn't. It was a strange feeling. What was I trained to do? And all of the pain and problems I had were still sitting there. I still didn't have a father; I still had management that I felt was sucking me dry. At least I had Nicollette. Maybe she would be the one who would give me strength to figure out what was next. There wasn't anybody else. Even a lot of my so-called friends seemed to be moving on once my star started fading. Little things I took for granted, like calls to play racquetball, all of a sudden weren't there. The invitations to parties became less frequent. Sure, my name still carried some sort of weight, but there certainly weren't going to be any more armored vehicles to deliver me from point A to point B.

I was drinking more and smoking more and doing whatever I could to numb the pain.

There was one more album with the Scottis, *My Movie of You,* which didn't do much of anything. I hit the PR circuit one last time to do a bunch of TV shows in Europe and some other countries, but the audiences were different. And I was getting older; I had my hair cut a little bit shorter. I was starting to look more like an adult, and this wasn't the material that was going to help me transition to the next level. This was more of the faceless, toothless, forgettable pop that I now had been making for years. This was going to do nothing but ensure the death of my recording career.

The record barely made the charts anywhere around the world. The single "Runaway Rita" reached only number eighty-four on the US charts. "Uptown Girl" did absolutely nothing. My five-year contract with the Scottis was almost up. The charade was, mercifully, almost over.

The Outsiders

I was losing control of everything, starting to seriously bottom out in the early '80s. But then I heard about this opportunity: a film audition for Francis Ford Coppola.

By the time I heard about the project, the audition process had already reached mythic proportions. Coppola was looking for the perfect cast to flesh out his cinematic adaptation of the classic coming-of-age S. E. Hinton novel *The Outsiders*. I flew to New York from London, and the moment I arrived early in the morning at the Joffrey Ballet School I knew the process would be unlike anything I'd ever experienced before. It was a cutthroat, relentless *Lord of the Flies* scenario that got tougher as the cuts were made. I'd never experienced a process as intense and unforgiving as this. Everybody watching who got cut, trading parts in endlessly changing groups; it was crazy. Elimination after elimination. But I hung in, Coppola seemed to like me, and then I received the call as I was headed back to Europe: *I'd gotten the part of Bob Sheldon*. Not because I was a teen idol. Not because I was a heartthrob. I had won the part. On my own. I had earned it, for being a good actor.

I would be joining the cast along with newcomers Tom Cruise, Rob Lowe, Emilio Estevez, Patrick Swayze, Matt Dillon, Ralph

Macchio, and C. Thomas Howell. The group represented the next important vanguard of young Hollywood actors, and I was part of it. I'd never been so proud or relieved in my life. Also in the film was the very cute Diane Lane, whom I'd met a few years earlier when her parents brought her to one of my concerts in New Jersey. She'd been a big fan and now we were working together, with more than a little flirting going on.

I became quite familiar with "The Silverfish," Coppola's legendary silver Airstream motor coach that housed a gourmet kitchen, an espresso machine, and a Jacuzzi, which he would often work from. The cold Tulsa, Oklahoma, nights were warmed nicely not just by his weed, but also by the wine he shared from his then new vineyards. (Incredibly, before filming the movie on thirty-five-millimeter film, Coppola spent two weeks around Tulsa filming the whole movie on videotape, to get a feel for how it would ultimately look. We made the movie twice!) When we shot my death scene, it was a cold Tulsa night, about three a.m., and we'd been shooting since dusk. I was soaking wet (I died after getting stabbed in the fountain), on the ground, freezing cold, and over the loudspeaker from Coppola's Silverfish I heard his "voice of God" say, "Cut. Leif, can you not shake so much? You're supposed to be dead."

This would be it, I thought. This film would revive my film career and save my post-teen idol ass.

During the shooting, I flew Nicollette in so we could be together. We missed each other, but in the end, it probably wasn't a good idea. When you're on location like that with lots of young people, there's lots of socializing going on. You're also working a lot. But she wanted to come visit. With Nicollette, we were either best friends in love or we cleared rooms. The situation in Tulsa was the latter. The minute she arrived, I think we knew it wasn't a good idea. It was distracting to me, and she certainly didn't seem happy either, without the attention she required. At a certain point she decided she was flying back to Los Angeles, but I said, "No, stay, let's work this out." But instead she went to Matt Dillon's room looking for money to take a taxi to the airport. She told him I was holding her hostage.

The day Nicollette left, I called Diane and asked her if she wanted to hang out. At that moment I really wanted to be with a beautiful woman without any drama. During the filming, I'd not been able to spend time with her the way I wanted to. I know I had not always been the perfect boyfriend. I still deeply loved Nicollette, but I hated the fighting. We were all still young; we were all still figuring things out. But I do wish I'd handled things better with Diane. I'll just leave that there.

For the record, I got decent reviews in *The Outsiders*. As I heard later, offers came in after from two different studios. But I never knew about them when they happened. Did the Scotti brothers drop the ball? Did my agents? I'll never know, I guess.

Money Talks

Look, we made good money with the Scotti brothers. But Marsa Hightower, before she left the company, expressed concern about the ethics of how our finances were being handled. She once called my mom privately into the ladies' room at the Scotti brothers' office and urged mom to ask questions about the books. My mom asked our business manager about Marsa's allegations, and he asked my mom, "Would she testify to that in court?" Mom went back and asked Marsa if she would, and was told no, she would not testify because it would end up costing her her career in the business. Sadly, Marsa is no longer alive and so we may never know why she made these accusations.

More John Belushi

Not long after things ended with the Scotti brothers, I was hunkered down in bungalow three at the Chateau Marmont hotel. John was thoroughly out of control at this point. He had come to LA to try to sell a screenplay, but the studio didn't like it, which pissed him off. I think that pushed him to do more of what he had been doing. So there I was, just twenty years old, doing blow with my pal John Belushi. *Tiger Beat* magazine should only have known what was going on. When I saw him throughout the week, I could tell things were bothering him. He wasn't his usual fun-loving self. He was doing more drugs than I remembered him doing, and his energy level had changed. He seemed tired. Things seemed to be catching up to him. He called me at home one day and told me to come over to the Chateau Marmont, where he was staying on that trip. I had been to the hotel a number of times to visit friends and for some parties but had not been in one of the private bungalows before. John was staying in number 103. The hotel sits back from Sunset Strip and is very private and quiet in a Gothic, even creepy sort of way. I love it there. The bungalows are even more secluded than the rest of the hotel, and the moment I found my way along the private path back to where John was staying, I knew things had changed for him. He had always done a lot of drugs and drank a lot, but there had always been a party atmosphere to him. He was loud and colorful. But on this night, the moment I entered the small bungalow, I could sense how things had taken a darker turn. Cocaine was being both smoked and snorted in the room, which was occupied by a handful of his friends, including some very famous ones. John put his arm around me and said, "How you been, kid?" He seemed out of it. His eyes were dead. Robin Williams was there, too, along with several other well-known people, everyone huddled up getting high together. They were kind of freaked, I think, that I was in the room. Sort of like, "Who is this guy?" But John assured them, "He's cool; it's okay. The kid is cool." Less than a week later, they would all be back in that same bungalow. Without me. That was the night John died in that room after a speed-ball was injected into him.

Part Three

AFTER

More Nicollette

The longer we lived together, the harder it became to maintain the magic of my relationship with Nicollette. We were on different paths at that point. My career was slowing down as hers was taking off. She was still amazing to be with. We still had plenty of good times, but I could sense that things were changing. As I've explained before, at that point we were either madly in love or we were clearing rooms. Both of our Scorpio emotions frequently got the better of us, but usually we came back together and made up—although by this point, the gaps were getting a little longer. We broke up a few times and wouldn't see each other for weeks. But there was always something about her that made me want to go back. And I always did. This wasn't just some girl. This was Nicollette. This was my goddess.

Roland Settlement

In December 1984, the Los Angeles Superior Court ordered my insurer, Transamerica Insurance Company, to pay $3.9 million to Roland Winkler. Jurors in the case assessed total damages in the civil negligence case at $4,215,500, but subtracted 8 percent of that amount, or $337,240, on the grounds that Roland had contributed to his own injuries by agreeing to ride in a car with a driver who he knew was drunk—namely, me. Yet Roland had been more out of it than I was, which is why I drove in the first place. Both of us admitted in court that we had been drunk and had taken depressant drugs; the court heard we had each taken equal amounts of alcohol and drugs that night, which actually was not even true. The panel ordered me to pay fifteen thousand dollars in punitive damages. Roland's attorney, Edward Steinbrecher, attributed the relatively small punitive damages award to my testimony that my net worth was only fifty thousand to one hundred thousand dollars. In 1987, Roland settled for six million dollars with the Premier Insurance Company, the insurer of the firm leasing the Porsche to my mom (it was in her name because I was a minor). I'm glad Roland was taken care of financially, but the horror of that night and what happened to him will never leave me.

Shaker Run and Nicollette Breakup

There were still some film parts for me. I starred in *Thunder Alley*, playing a singer, of all things. (I was happy to have won the audition by actually singing—imagine!) Next up was *Shaker Run*, which was shot in New Zealand. I played a stunt car driver along with Cliff Robertson. Before I headed off, I had done a lot of soul-searching about Nicollette. I wanted to spend the rest of my life with her. It was that simple. I never wanted to lose her again. We were always going through these mini breakups and I, in my selfishness, would automatically go off and find comfort elsewhere during the time we were apart. She hated that, just like I did when she behaved the same way. I was tired of that behavior. I was twenty-four years old, and she was twenty-two. I wanted to propose to Nicollette, and I wanted it to be special.

Once I arrived in New Zealand, I began making arrangements to pop the question to Nicollette. I then flew her down there, under the cover story that I missed her and wanted her down there for a little vacation. I had a Jeroboam Moët & Chandon champagne waiting for her in Queenstown in my hotel suite overlooking the water and the snow-covered mountains. I had bought her a beautiful half-carat diamond and I secretly put the diamond in a champagne flute, carefully filling the glass only halfway. We toasted, but to my shock, she knocked the champagne back like she was doing a shot. The rock must have hit a tooth, and she said, "What the hell...?" and I pointed out the diamond in the glass and said to her, "Will you marry me?" There was a huge pause. She looked me lovingly in the eyes and said, "Yes, I will marry you." It was the special moment I was looking for. And then we spent a blissful night together. She was with me for about a week, and thankfully I had some time off from shooting so that we could make a real vacation of it. We took a helicopter ride with Cliff Robertson; we went on a jet boat excursion and took long romantic walks together. It was wonderful.

The night before she left to go back home (I had a couple of weeks left to shoot), I basically told Nicollette everything I'd done in my life. Everyone I'd been with, every crazy sexual situation—everything. She wanted to know, and I shared it with her because I wanted to come clean. I wanted her to know everything about me so that we could both move on together without any baggage. And then she left.

A couple of days after she got home, I woke up in the middle of the night after having had a nightmare about us. I couldn't recall the exact details, but in the dream she was leaving me. The dream was too real to ignore, so I picked up the phone and called her at her friend Vicky's house, where she was staying. She had recently moved out of my house because we'd decided it would be good for both of us to have a little space. I felt very scared as the phone rang. It was as if I had experienced an omen. Vicky answered the phone. I said right away, "Vicky, can I please speak to Nicollette? There was a pause. "She is sleeping," Vicky answered. "Can you please wake her up?" "Leif, she told me, she wants to sleep." This wasn't making sense. "Vicky, come on, you know me. Can you please help me out here? Can I please speak to Nicollette?" I knew Vicky well enough to know she was holding something back. We went back and forth a couple of times, I started to lose it, and she finally blurted, "She's not here, Leif."

My heart sank. "Where is she?" I asked.

"She's at Tim's."

"Tim who?"

"Tim Hutton."

I couldn't believe it. I had recently been partying with Tim, Sean Penn, and a few other guys. I had actually introduced Tim to Nicollette not long before. I felt like the ground fell away under my feet. She had just accepted my proposal. How could she do this? I had poured my heart out to her. I needed to get home right away. I went to the production people and told them I had to go home to deal with an emergency. They thought I was crazy. Barring something like a death in the family, I could not leave them high and dry, so I finished up my work in the next few days. In one stunt scene that I was doing myself, I crashed into one of the cameras and got a big gash on my head. I was a mess. I wasn't thinking clearly. I had to get home.

When I finally got back to Los Angeles a couple of days later, I went right to her apartment but Nicollette was not there. I started making phone calls all over town, but I could not locate her. This was worse than what I was feeling in New Zealand because I was now so close and yet so far. I drove out to Malibu and knocked on Timothy Hutton's door. When he answered, I said to him, "Is Nicollette here?" He looked very surprised, fumbled for a moment, and said, "Why would she be here?" Okay, fine. Now I was just getting lied to. The next several days were so dark and so bleak, I didn't know what to do with myself. When I did finally find Nicollette and talk to her, it was like my worst nightmare coming true. In short, she explained to me that after hearing me talk to her about all that I had done in life, she had thought about it on the way home and decided that there were still plenty of things that she wanted to do. Right away I regretted pouring my heart out to her. She wanted to have all of the experiences that I had had. My coming clean with her was an awakening for her. And so she reconsidered her promise to me, and that was it. That was it for good. There was no more Nicollette in my life. And I had never felt as bad as I did when I finally realized that it was over. I needed to self-medicate. Badly.

Not long after the breakup with Nicollette, I was down in Florida to play in a celebrity tennis tournament. The brothers Jimmy and Vince Van Patten were also playing. I knew Vince because we had done the TV show *Three for the Road* together. I didn't know Jimmy that well, yet I poured my heart out to both of them about Nicollette and how shattered I was. What I didn't know is that she had also been sleeping with Jimmy Van Patten. Those guys didn't say a word to me. They let me go on and on, and I looked like such a fool. I felt like everybody was letting me down. Why do I trust so few people today? Gee, I wonder.

The Road to Freedom: Scientology

The breakup with Nicollette was devastating for me. As I've said, we had broken up before, many times, but I had always known in the back of my mind that it wasn't the very end. That was the rhythm of our relationship. But this was different. She was gone, and I knew she was gone for good. She was spreading her wings—like I had done—and she obviously had fallen in love with somebody else. The first few months after the breakup were some of the hardest I have ever experienced. I felt hollow. I was completely lost. It was a complete, total, and devastating loss for me. Not only had I lost the love of my life, but at that point my career had essentially sputtered into almost nothing. I had watched Nicollette grow as an actress, and I knew the future she had in front of her. Me? It was like I was finished. Twenty-five years old, and I felt like I had nothing to live for. My entire existence had been completely altered. The world just did not seem the same without Nicollette. Had I done something wrong? Was it my fault? In hindsight, I think we were just too young for that kind of permanent relationship. But back then, in the moment, I was heartbroken on levels I never thought I could experience.

It's during those times, I think, when one is so lost, that one becomes vulnerable to those who want to take advantage. I don't think I was thinking clearly when I got a call from Joel Stevens. He was an industry guy, a showbiz manager I'd met years earlier at the John Denver Celebrity Ski Tournament. And he was a Scientologist. There was always something about Scientologists—it was if they knew when you were at your lowest point. They knew when it was the right time to move in. Joel's radar must have been up because he called me and told me that an album was being made, songs based on the writings of L. Ron Hubbard. He was excited: "Leif, I think this would be perfect for you. You're a good singer, and look at who's involved with this: John Travolta, Chick Corea; other great names. This would be good for you. This will help you get out of your funk. You don't look well. You need help, and I think maybe Scientology can give it to you."

Joel knew how to recruit for Scientology. He knew I was in a lot of pain after breaking up with Nicollette. He also knew I had just suffered a devastating motorcycle accident. It was a bad one. I had been riding my BMW R65 on Wilshire Boulevard near Comstock Avenue, coming down from the Beverly Glen neighborhood. I was about to hit a red light; it turned green, and a lady coming toward me started making a left but instead of committing, she stopped. I smashed right into her, ripped my knees open, and flew over the bike. I think people thought I was dead. I was badly banged up but I was okay, miraculously. The bike was totally trashed. I did a full-on 360-degree flip. It was the only time in my life that I actually saw my life pass before my eyes in split-second vignettes. Everything became compressed in the blink of an eye: acting as a little child, my father screaming, my first concert, all of the women, everything in the blink of an eye. Believe it or not, today I still have that motorcycle. I had it crushed into a coffee table; it's a perfect square with a piece of beveled glass on top. Sometimes I need reminders of where I've been.

Anyway, Joel knew all of these things. He sensed I was a broken person—not just physically but also emotionally and spiritually. I was exactly what Scientologists prey on. "Now is the time, Leif," he said to me. "You have to get out there and show everyone what you believe in. We're going to give you something to believe. This is a big moment for you. It's going to help you."

Scientology in the 1980s was a lot different than it is today, or at least the perception of it was. Back then it still had a lot of mystique. It wasn't looked at as a predatory cult, but rather more of a self-help mechanism, not that different from things like est, primal scream therapy, or other newfangled, new-age practices. One thing L. Ron Hubbard knew early in the game, and this was very smart of him, is that attaching celebrities to his "religion" would not just give his "church" credibility, but also make it something that regular people would aspire to be a part of. I was a celebrity, and I knew that's why Joel was talking to me. But I was also in a weakened state. I needed something, but I didn't know what. I agreed to sing on the record.

I drove out to the dusty city of Hemet, about two hours southeast of LA by car, onto the mysterious Scientology campus and into a building shaped like a yacht. There were zombies everywhere—that is, people wandering around who looked devoid of any true human emotions; robotic and programmed. John Travolta and the others would be adding their parts to the record later. Today it was just me. L. Ron Hubbard had just died, but in his personal recording studio and offices, it was as if he'd never left. Everything was still in place, and the people there spoke about him in the present tense as if he were still watching over them. Were they going to pay me a lot of money for being on the record? No. That album eventually went platinum in countries all over the world, and of course I never saw a penny from it. I got a Scientology T-shirt and a couple of classes (I actually liked the communications class a lot), and that was about it. I still had no idea how to make deals that would protect me. Back in Los Angeles, where I began taking the classes, I saw Tom Cruise, John Travolta, and several other celebrities who were able to use the VIP areas of the "church." I also experienced the "Purification" process—a combination of Niacin, exercise, and dry sauna. Joining me in the sauna at various times were Brad Pitt, Juliette Lewis, and Tom Berenger, among others. I'm not saying these actors were all Scientologists; they were just experimenting, like me.

One day in the dining room there, I also saw the new leader of Scientology. He was an intense, short guy named David Miscavige. I sat at his table briefly, and there was something very off-putting about him. He seemed like a dictator. He was barking orders at people and seemed quite unpleasant. Ultimately, I had no real place in Scientology. The auditing and the whole e-meter thing I found (and still find) to be totally ridiculous. I knew I was not going to belong to Scientology. But I wish I had known how much that album was going to sell within the church. I have a framed photo at home of me recording the album, but that's about it. I think if people had realized then what many now think Miscavige was doing—that is, taking over with a brutally dictatorial approach—Scientology wouldn't have found itself in the shape it is today, with people leaving the church and getting attacked for exiting. I say thanks to brave former members like Leah Remini, who have committed themselves to exposing some obviously despicable behavior. Look, I try to never make judgments about what people believe in, what they worship, or where their faith lies. Those are very personal and private matters. But when any organization begins strong-arming people simply because they want to leave and begins threatening them with exposing personal information, well, then I have a problem.

Once I was out of Scientology, I still didn't have anyplace else to go. There was no Nicollette and not a lot of work. All that lay ahead for me was a burgeoning Hollywood scene featuring lots of young stars collectively known as "the Brat Pack." I became a fringe member of that group, doing whatever I could, appearing in a slew of embarrassing low-budget disasters, just to ensure that I had money for drugs.

Justine Bateman

Istarted dating the actress Justine Bateman in the late 1980s. It was a much different situation than it had been with Nicollette—an entirely different sort of relationship altogether, but I liked it and I think it's what I needed at that point. Justine was an activist and very intellectual. She was serious, and I liked that. She was politically active, so I got involved in a variety of causes. This was new ground for me, and I was enjoying it. We went to the 1988 Democratic convention in Atlanta. We met with lawmakers as part of the bold new Hollywood set that was becoming active in government affairs. But along with the public political gravitas there was still lots of socializing and other craziness happening behind the scenes. As you may remember, Rob Lowe ran into some trouble after videotaping himself in a hotel room with two girls. They wound up taking the tape, and the next day, before all hell broke loose, Rob told a small group of us—myself, Justine, and Judd Nelson, among a few others—that he felt he had "really screwed up." It wound up being one of the first true celebrity scandals in the brand-new home video age.

Justine was a big star as a result of appearing on the hit show *Family Ties* as Mallory Keaton. As a result, oftentimes when we were in public, she would get approached for autographs. She didn't

With Justine and Michael J. I love them both.

always like dealing with that, especially if we were in a restaurant or something. On the one hand, I understood her concern about being interrupted. But I would also try to explain to her, "Look, these are your fans; these are the ones that make all of this possible. Even if it becomes slightly inconvenient, it's not a good idea to ever say no to a genuine fan." That had always been my approach. The fans mattered and needed to be treated that way.

This was a time when celebrity culture was getting out of hand though. We were invited to the wedding of Michael J. Fox, which was held in 1988 at the exclusive West Mountain Inn in Arlington, Vermont. Obviously, a lot of celebrities were going to be in attendance, and a well-known tabloid offered me a small spy camera to take a photo of the wedding, for which it would pay something like two hundred thousand dollars. I couldn't believe it. Honestly, there was no amount of money anyone could pay me to violate someone's privacy like that. It disgusted me. But it pointed toward the future. People were becoming so obsessed with celebrities that it was getting to things like this.

Eventually, I moved in with Justine, and we lived together for about a year. We had a nice time together. I loved feeling her hold on when riding on the back of my motorcycle (we were always riding in packs with good friends like former Sex Pistol Steve Jones), and all in all I think it was a good relationship that we both needed. We started growing apart though because we were both reaching crossroads in our lives. When *Family Ties* ended its massively popular run in 1989, Justine was thinking about her future, obviously, and I was thinking of how to reinvent myself, more in the musical realm than acting. We drifted apart as we looked ahead, but it was a relationship I remember with deep fondness.

Jason Bateman Road Trip

My friend, Peter Morgan, Jason Bateman, and I planned a trip to Colorado for New Year's in 1990. It was going to be a real "guys" road trip. We were going to rent a motor home and stock it with good wine, good weed, and, of course, our skis. At the last minute, Peter bailed, but that wasn't going to slow down Jason and me. So off we went to Aspen.

I have always loved a good road trip, anything to escape all of the prying eyes that existed so close to home wherever I went, even in the afterglow of having been a teen idol. Getting out on the road gave me my only real sense of freedom. This specific road trip idea was hatched over one of our weekly poker games. First we headed up north to ski in Squaw Valley, then it was on to Park City and Deer Valley in Utah. It was crazy and debauched, with some of the best skiing of our lives.

Our thirty-five-foot Winnebago was as chaotic as you might have expected. When we hit Aspen, it was just in time for Jack Nicholson's New Year's party. We couldn't park a thirty-five-foot motor home in front of any of the Victorian mansions, so we found a spot alongside the river, and nobody said a word for the whole two weeks we were there. We had the time of our lives. We hung out at Don Johnson's place after New Year's, and I got to see a lot of old actor and musician friends. Justine came into town and joined us too. I have such great memories of Aspen. A year or so before, I had been frequenting a restaurant in Aspen. One night, the door opened up and in walked the gonzo writer Hunter S. Thompson. I was a huge fan. Kind of bizarrely, he was wearing shorts and tube socks and tennis shoes in the dead of winter. "Dude," I said to him after noticing the circular Deering grinder he used to chop up his coke, stashed in his sock, "you might want to put a hockey puck in your pocket." "Do you partake?" he asked me. A few minutes later we were in the bathroom getting high together. Hunter and I became friends out there and even wound up playing paddle tennis a few times. I went to his infamous house in Woody Creek, Colorado, and it was awesome getting to hang out with him. He was a huge sports fan, funny as hell and, of course, a little bit crazy. So, of course, I looked him up when Jason and I went through.

Jason and I drove back to California, wiped out, weary, but both of us with big smiles on our faces. It was one of the greatest road trips of my life.

Heroin

I could handle the drinking. I could handle the cocaine. I could handle the Quaaludes. The heroin was a whole other story. If I could go back and change one thing in my life—just one thing—I would've not started using heroin. It never should have started, and I have always felt a bit tricked as to how it did start, at least as a habit. Technically, I did it once by accident at Studio 54 years earlier, but my habit happened more by design. There was a dealer I knew, Ed, and he was told by his source that he could make a lot more money if he dealt more than just coke and weed; that if he dealt heroin, it would be far more profitable. To start the business off, he would need to get people around him hooked. Basically give it away for a week to get people hooked, and then he would have us all as customers.

One day he asked if I wanted to smoke some opium. I should've known better. Maybe I was looking for it, I don't know. I was so down at this point in my life that I wasn't thinking that clearly. Heroin is very good business, and I think this guy knew it. I know a lot of people who got hooked when he started dealing. Anyway, he called it opium, I smoked it, and within three days that stuff owned me. The way it goes is, you wake up after three days and you're a heroin addict. You are a junkie. And it set my life on a course that ultimately did more damage to me than anything else.

It happened so quickly. I didn't have a lot of cash coming in at that point, and soon I was smoking about three hundred dollars' worth a day at my worst. I wanted to be numb. I wanted to forget everything. I had a hard time dealing with what had happened to my career. I was a lost soul. I started pawning things at first. Then I began selling everything I had. I had to. But I never stole anything from anyone. I probably smoked more than one million dollars' worth of heroin (I have been scared of needles my whole life). That's how bad it was. Every single day became the same, one sickening blur from one day to the next. Wake up, have your dealer deliver the goods, smoke, repeat the next day. It's all I thought about. I would occasionally get called out to read for a movie, and I ended up in lots of garbage little films. I didn't care about my career anymore. I cared about heroin. Heroin became everything to me.

Night with
Robert Downey Jr.

As some of you might remember, Robert Downey Jr. and I ran together a lot back in the late 1980s through the mid-1990s. I always found Robert to be very funny and, of course, very talented. I'm incredibly impressed by how he reinvented himself and became one of the most popular actors of today. It's a remarkable turnaround when you think back to how things were back in the day. We had so much fun, but of course the damages took their toll. It was a crazy time. There were many nights we spent both together and with people we were dating (or in his case, married to), and I have fond memories of a lot of those experiences. There were also times when things would get woefully out of control, and I could probably write an entirely separate book about all of those nights spent with Robert and other young actors and entertainers who all got caught up in the madness of the Hollywood drug culture.

But I'm not writing this memoir to catalog every single one of those experiences. For one thing, I think it would get old fast. And for another, I'm sure I can't remember most of them, given how hard we were all hitting it back then. But one night remains vividly etched into my memory; it wound up being a blend of tragedy and comedy, and it sort of exemplifies just how over the top everything was getting.

In the mid-1990s, the industrial band Orgy had recently signed a record deal, and to celebrate we had a party up at Matt Sorum's house in the Hollywood Hills. Matt was then the drummer for Guns N' Roses, and he was a cool guy and a great player. A lot of musicians were hanging out with actors then, each fascinated with the other. As I recall, the house (formerly Madonna's) was a very cool space and was a great place to make music in. There was a studio downstairs, and a bunch of us were hanging out: the guys from Orgy, Matt, Mark McGrath, and Robert and his wife Debbie, among others.

Debbie had gone into the bathroom and didn't come out for a long time. Robert started banging on the door, and there was no answer. I climbed in through an outside window and shockingly, found Debbie on the floor having some kind of seizure. I wasn't sure what exactly had happened. We were all doing a lot of drugs—cocaine, smoking heroin, and drinking. It appeared she had fallen forward and hit her head on the sink. But I wasn't sure. All I knew was that we needed help and needed it fast. "Call 911!" I yelled out. But right away Robert tried to assure me she was okay. "She'll be fine. We don't need to call anybody. Don't move her." Matt started freaking out: "Oh my god, nobody say a word. Get her out of here! We need to clear the space up right now!" Then he ran out of the room. In fact, everybody started leaving, quickly. The guys from Orgy bolted; Mark McGrath bolted—it was just me, Robert, and Debbie left in the bathroom. She started coming to, but she was groggy. "Debbie, how many fingers am I holding up?" I asked her. "Eighteen." Things were not looking good, and I still wanted to call 911. I wasn't going to let her die. Addicts get very paranoid. Nobody wants to call the law; nobody wants to call paramedics; nobody wants anybody official entering the scene. I totally understood this and have been there many times myself. But for some reason, that night I had my wits about me, and I knew we needed to help this woman or else. So I made the call. Within minutes, an ambulance pulled up to the house, and both Robert and I were nervous as two female paramedics came in to try to resuscitate Debbie. Would they recognize us? Thankfully neither one of them did. They were there to focus on the problem at hand, and that made things easier. One hassle avoided.

When they loaded Debbie into the ambulance, they asked Robert if he wanted to ride along. He said no, which really surprised me. "That's your wife, man. You have to go with them." "No, no, no," he assured me. "This will be okay. We will follow up in my car." I should have known Robert had something else on his mind. We got into his Audi, me behind the wheel because Robert was so fucked up, and started following the ambulance to City of Angels Hospital on Vermont Avenue. "You should be in that ambulance, man," I said to him. But he had other plans. I saw him on his cell phone, and I said, "What are you doing?"

"We've got to pick something up."

"Are you fucking kidding me?"

Look, I was an addict too. But there was a time and a place for everything. This was not the time to be scoring. But I gave up. He called our dealer and told him we were coming by to pick up an eight-ball. But it didn't stop there. He also wanted to stop at a liquor store to pick up some vodka and orange juice. I pulled in to a minimart where I saw a liquor store, and I went in to get what he wanted. Me, I was just craving a Yoo-hoo. This is probably a good point in the story to tell you that I believe this was the only night in my life I was wearing white jeans. When I got in the car and started driving back toward the hospital, I shook the Yoo-hoo up before drinking it but forgot I had opened it already. My pants all of a sudden were covered with the brown liquid, and it looked like I had shat myself.

We finally arrived at the hospital, and I said to Robert, "Come on," as I got out of the car. He refused. "They will recognize me in there. You go inside and see what's going on. Then come get me." This was getting stupider by the second. But he was my friend, and I did what he asked of me. This was me all over, I'm telling you. I did pretty much whatever anybody wanted, when they wanted, sometimes putting all common sense aside. Anyway, I walked into the hospital, found the emergency room admittance desk, and asked where Debbie Downey was. "Get in here quickly!" she said. "Obviously something has happened to you!" "Leave me alone," I said. "I'm fine. I'm just trying to find out what room she's in." They were reacting to the Yoo-hoo stains on my white jeans. I explained that I was fine, and the scene got crazier.

They wouldn't tell me where Debbie was because I was not a family member, and I explained to them that her husband was in the car, that he would come in in a moment, but could they please be low-key if they recognized who he was? They seemed to understand, so I went back outside to fetch him. When I got back out there, I felt like I was watching an outtake from the film *Scarface*. Robert had white powder all over his face; obviously he hadn't told me in the car that he had been holding out. He finally got his shit together and went inside the hospital, and Debbie was ultimately okay. Robert and I reconnected later that night, and he seemed genuinely relieved that she was okay. That made me feel better. But this was the kind of thing that would happen with me and my friends all the time. And trust me, I was as bad as any of them. The amount of drugs we were doing was becoming so out of control that we were literally risking our lives and the lives of our loved ones on a regular basis. Again, I'm very proud that Robert cleaned himself up, did his time, and went on to create the career that he has. It's a great example that it's never too late. And I think it's something we all can learn from.

Elaine

I had been friends with Elaine Bilstad for a number of years in the early 1990s, along with her then-boyfriend, Daniel Bardol. She was very pretty and, of course, I was attracted to her, but still we had just been friends. She would try to connect me with girlfriends of hers, and once in a while it would work, but not for long. Eventually Elaine and I developed a relationship, and I fell deeply in love with her. It was different than being with Nicollette. Being good friends first and then having things develop into a relationship was a new thing for me, and I liked it.

Elaine was an actress. We would go out to parties and things with Robert and Debbie Downey, who were her friends, too, but we also spent a lot of time alone together. We would go camping together out in the desert at Joshua Tree and places like that. That was Elaine. She loved being outdoors and had a very natural way about her. Sadly for both of us, that was right around the time I started doing heroin. What had started as a lovely little love affair soon became corrupted by the drug.

When the addiction kicked in, I was going through a lot of money for the both of us. Soon Elaine and I occasionally went to flea markets on weekends selling things of mine to make money. We'd make candles, copper crosses, and other crafts to sell. It was hard. Neither of us was working steadily so money was always tight. Eventually she would leave me because of heroin. She couldn't take my addiction anymore, and I don't blame her. At that point I barely had a place to live. I would crash at friends' houses on couches or even sleep under a table in my mom's apartment. I was so close to being homeless that it wasn't even funny. I had nothing. No money, and soon no Elaine; my dream of our being a young couple with all of our dreams ahead of us evaporated, burned away like so much brown powder on the foil. She was my best friend and I missed her beyond measure. I was starting to feel like the end of my life was near. I would've been okay had I died at that point; I would've had no complaints. I had lived a very full and complete life, and I hated what I had become.

In my possession today, I have a framed piece of silver foil. Spelled out in the residue of the heroin I was so addicted to is the word "help." I made it by shaping the residue on the foil into the letters. That was my cry for help. But nobody ever got to read that. I was sitting by myself in my room, lost and lonely, living the life of a junkie. Several years later, Ed, the guy who had gotten me hooked, came to my door and mentioned, almost flippantly, that he had heard that Elaine had died recently, from a heart ailment. This pushed me even deeper into the abyss.

This was how I used to do it. I have always had a great fear of needles! Just promise me you will never try it!

For Elaine
South Africa, 1995

Oh delicate rose
So strong, so proud
Standing tall with morning's dew on your tender lips
Unfold your petals to the sun and let me breathe in your scent
Radiant as the loving moon
Shine with the beauty most can only dream of
I wish to be the one
The one to hold you
As your thorns pierce my common flesh
To remind me of your fiery soul
My garden awaits and craves you
Open arms and open heart
With soil as rich as the blood you let
Oh beautiful rose
Oh beautiful rose

—Leif

Working in a Bike Shop

For about a year I went up to Tahoe City, California, and worked in my cousin Peter's bicycle shop. I had nothing much to do. I barely had a place to live, as mentioned, bouncing around from couch to couch, doing the odd carpentry job here and there for some cash. I was battling my heroin addiction and simply took my bad habit up there with me. There were some people down in LA who would travel up north to deliver drugs to me, and I know that Peter was confused about my behavior. He was a pretty straight arrow, and I know it never made sense to him when I would nod off or disappear unexpectedly for hours at a time. But he always stuck by me and gave me something to do at the shop.

There was a girl who worked there along with me. She was a few years younger than me, local, and she was cool to work with. That was her life up there. One day we were cleaning up the shop. I forget how the conversation started, but we started talking about the 1970s and people who had been popular back then. I had just met her, and she didn't even know my name. So we were talking about things we used to do when we were teenagers, and she started telling me, "I think my biggest obsession as a teenager was *Leef* Garrett." When I said to her, "I think his name was pronounced *Lafe* Garrett," she said, "Okay, *Lafe*

Garrett. I was obsessed with him. I had his pictures all over my walls. I read all the fan magazines. He's all I thought about. It's funny what we do when we are young." I almost didn't know what to say. I guess I had changed that much. She didn't even know that the object of her affection was standing right next to her. She didn't believe me at first when I revealed who I was. Then she hugged me, and Peter came in at that point, laughing. It was nice to be reminded of what I once had been.

Intervention

In a 1999 episode of the VH1 documentary series *Behind the Music*, the 1996 intervention that was staged by my family and friends was a big part of the show. For the most part, it was described accurately, but there was a lot more to it. And there were things I have learned about it since then. Everybody was tired of watching me disintegrate. I don't think there's anything much worse than watching someone you care about suffer the ravages of heroin addiction. That was my entire life. I woke up in the morning with one thought and one thought only: *Where will I get the money to buy today's batch?* I would look for a couple of things to sell, go unload them at a pawnshop or someplace, and then go score. Or call and have the stuff delivered. By the time of the intervention, I was smoking about three hundred dollars' worth of black tar heroin a day. It was all I had in the world. Heroin addiction is so all-consuming, it can hardly be accurately described. Every penny you have goes to the drug. Nothing is okay until you have the drug. It owns you completely. Being in the abyss of heroin addiction is a bleak, lonely, and desperate existence.

By now I had a little apartment on Third Street, and I lived in my bedroom with my two dogs. I loved those two, Sequoia and Cochise. They didn't judge me; they were there to look out for me and take care of me. But even they looked at me with sad eyes. My skin was rotting. I was dying right in front of them, disintegrating. The only thing I had going for me was a roof over my head, and it was probably only a matter of time before I lost that. I was broke; I was broken. I would sit in my dark bedroom, fixing my heroin, "chasing the dragon," as it's called when you inhale those deadly (but seductive) vapors, nodding off until I started it all over again—a vicious and sickening cycle that I wouldn't wish on anybody. I was simply preparing to die in that little room. I would look back on my life and think about my mistakes. Think about the opportunities I had squandered. Think about the fact that I never had a father figure to talk to or help counsel me. Think about so many things that I couldn't change. I did not want to live anymore, so I was killing myself with heroin.

There are times in life when you have to wonder if there's an angel watching over you. I had no idea that Nicollette was going to call my cousin Peter. I hadn't seen Peter in so long. We had nothing to talk about anymore. I had idolized him, and I knew that I had let him down. He was also going through a tough divorce and had his own personal issues. Nobody had time for me, and I didn't blame them. He had to take care of his own issues. But evidently Nicollette contacted him and said, "Our boy needs our help." She had gotten word about how serious my condition had become, from a former friend, I'm guessing. And so Peter and Nicollette gathered one morning in my apartment with a group of my friends and family. I had no idea ahead of time. All I knew was there was a knock on my bedroom door and all of a sudden, magically, there was Peter. It was like a dream. I could see in his eyes that he couldn't believe what he was looking at. My bedroom looked like what it was, a squalid junkie crash pad. He tried to put a bright spin on it. "Hey, bro, I was down here on business and thought I would buy you breakfast." This seemed kind of strange. He rousted me out of bed a little too enthusiastically, and we walked downstairs to the kitchen. Our conversation was awkward as he started fixing coffee, and as he walked into the other room for a second, the door leading from the kitchen into the living room—a swinging door—revealed, for a split second, a roomful of people. At least I thought it did. It was like an illusion. *Is that my mom in there? My friend Steve Jones from the Sex Pistols? Singer Michael Des Barres? And who is that strange guy I have never seen?*

All of a sudden it hit me: This was an intervention.

I didn't want to overreact, so I calmly told Peter I needed to run up to my room for a second. I went up there, locked the door, and smoked what little heroin I had left. I kissed my dogs goodbye, climbed out the window, shimmied down the fire escape, and walked about two blocks to a gas station where there was a pay phone. I dialed my number, knowing everyone in my apartment would hear the answering machine go off on speaker. "Get the fuck out of my house!" I yelled at them. "I am calling the police if you're not out of my house in one minute." I couldn't believe what was happening. I was not a good candidate for an intervention at that time.

When I got back to my apartment, everybody was gone except my mother, Nicollette, and Peter. Nicollette. She was beautiful. Had she really done this for me? Was she still concerned? Would we get back together? Was there any hope? My brain rattled with a series of crazy questions. My god, she was still so stunning. My mother couldn't stop crying, and Peter comforted her, but Nicollette was focused. "Come on," she said. "We are going someplace to get help for you." I couldn't resist. If Nicollette was telling me this, then I believed her. Maybe there was still hope. That's all I cared about in that moment. Looking at her, I flashed back to all of those moments we had spent together. That day I first saw her at the party. That morning when Brad showed up and took our photo. Everything. I still cared about her so much.

I packed my bag and got into her car. She told me she was taking me to someplace in Pasadena. I tried making small talk with her, but she was very businesslike. It was as if she couldn't stand to look at me. I guess I could understand why. I looked awful. I was repulsive. We got to the hospital and I was checked in. I asked Nicollette when I could see her again, and she told me to do what they said and that she would see me soon. She stressed, "You need to do this, Leif." And with that, she was gone.

A stern, steely-eyed nurse let me into a cold little room that seemed more like a jail cell than anything else. I was thinking, *Gone are the days of the rooftop suite at the Dorchester. This is your life now, buddy. Get used to it.* Well, you know what? I couldn't get used to it. I had to get out of there. After about ten minutes, I tiptoed out of the room and went to find a pay phone. I called a taxi and told the guy to meet me at the bottom of the hill near the hospital. Then I snuck back in my room, loaded up my duffel bag, and crept out the front door. Nobody saw me. Not a word was said. It was that easy. I was back home within about half an hour, back in bed with my dogs, smoking the rest of the heroin stash I had left. I will never forget what Nicollette did in trying to help me, but I simply wasn't ready.

Look, I'm a very stubborn person who doesn't like being told what to do. And if you plan something behind my back like that, well, let's just say I also don't like surprises. Looking back, I appreciate what everyone did that night, especially Nicollette, but the timing wasn't right. I know it sounds like I'm making excuses, and maybe I am. I wish it had been the right time. I wish I had been more open-minded. I wish I had had the strength to at least try kicking heroin that night. Because it was only about to get worse. Much worse.

Reunion?

I walked into Coco's restaurant in Santa Monica, and I barely recognized him sitting alone in the booth. My father. I had not seen him for about twenty years. The last time he and I had been together was when he visited me in the hospital back when everybody thought I was sick, when they canceled my tour due to lack of sales. I had not seen him since then. He missed my childhood, he missed my teenage years, and he also missed me in my twenties. And here I was in my mid-thirties. I wasn't in the best of shape. I was struggling. He looked the same, just a lot older. I forget how it had happened exactly, but I think he contacted my sister about wanting to get together with each of us. Just out of the blue. There was no real cause for it. Neither of us had very much to say. I wanted to ask him, "Where were you? Why weren't you there to watch us grow up?" But I knew there was no answer that would satisfy me. I think he was curious about who we were, what we looked like, and what we were doing. I don't know if he was aware that I had a drug problem. If he was, he didn't say anything.

There's not much more to say about this meeting. Even in the state that I was in, I still felt very sad for what we had lost. My father sat there trying to blame my mother for the situation. He started saying to me that my mother had been too possessive of me, and that had made it hard for him. I know that both of my parents have their own points of view about what happened to our family. But as one of the kids who was affected by both of their actions, I felt sad sitting in the booth. It reminded me that I never had a father figure and how much I probably could've used one. Today, as my father's primary caregiver, I have many mixed emotions. I take care of him because he's my father. No matter how badly he may have treated us, he's still my father. And in the back of my mind, buried deep, are the yearnings of a little boy who wants nothing more than his father to call him over, tap on the side of the bed for him to sit down, and have a heart-to-heart talk about life. I don't think I will ever get that. And that's okay. I've accepted him for who he is. But still, as the shadows grow, I still feel so desperate for that moment. Maybe someday.

1997: Dave Navarro, Billy Zane, Marilyn Manson

I had started hanging out with the actor Billy Zane, and he introduced me to Marilyn Manson. We spent many late nights hanging out in Marilyn's house up in Laurel Canyon, along with Marilyn's bassist, Twiggy, and many other interesting characters. There were obviously a lot of drugs, but also a lot of music and good times. It was always fun hanging out with those guys. I appreciated Marilyn and what he was doing as an artist. He was pushing boundaries and constantly reinventing himself, not unlike what Bowie had done a couple of decades earlier—and I have always been a huge Bowie fan.

I fit in up at the house in kind of a strange way. All those guys—Marilyn, Dave Navarro, Nikki Sixx—they didn't like my music from way back when, but I didn't either. But they did all seem to appreciate the style I had brought back then. To these guys, I was a type of pop culture icon whom they appreciated. They remembered all of the magazines and the craziness, and that was interesting to them. And, of course, my reputation with women was something everybody always wanted to hear about as well. They always asked me questions about the old days, about what it was like to be so hot and so wildly popular. They were just really into pop culture.

Hanging around them got me thinking about music again and about what I wanted to be doing. Eventually, a number of us would all work together on my solo project, but when I first started hanging out up there, it was just a chance to enter a new world I felt comfortable in. All of these guys were making good music on their own terms. I liked that. That inspired me. It also helped me come to grips with what I had been years before. I think in a way I was trying to shed my skin with them, so in sort of a ceremonial act, I began giving them my gold records. They all freaked out and thought they were receiving some great cultural artifacts. But to me it was part of a life that was fake. I didn't want those things around me anymore. I gave Twiggy one; Dave got one; I also gave one to my friend Julian Raymond for his efforts to try and produce a hit song for me that we cowrote.

At a certain point, the Rock & Roll Hall of Fame in Cleveland had an exhibit dedicated to teen idols, and asked if I could lend them a few of my things. I asked Marilyn if I could have the records back for a short period to be put on display. I assured him I would give them back to him after the exhibit closed. But he took it the wrong way and called me an "Indian giver." Sadly, that was the end of our friendship.

1997: Chris Farley

I don't know why anybody does drugs. As far as what drove me to start doing hard drugs like heroin, I think it was a combination of three things. First, my dysfunctional family. When you are told at eight years old that you're basically in charge of providing for the household, that's a lot of pressure. I always wished for parents to raise me and nurture me and guide me. I never got that. To this day I take care of both of my parents, and I'm still trying to have the relationship I always wanted to have. But I have some resentments too.

The second factor is that I was trapped being a teen idol. The tension and frustration of not being able to do what I wanted artistically, I think, finally wore me down and left me vulnerable. I hated the stuff the Scotti brothers had made for me to sing. I wanted to rock out. I wanted to experiment with songs I learned about over in Europe before they made their way to America. But I wasn't allowed to. I considered myself somewhat of a fraud (even if the only untruths were how much I liked the music I was doing and that I was the only one singing on the first three records).

The third factor is that I thought that to be a legitimate rock star, I had to take hard drugs and live the rock 'n' roll lifestyle.

These still are the three basic themes of my life. As to why other performers and entertainers fall prey to addiction, I don't know. But I sure managed to connect with a lot of them.

Chris Farley always kind of reminded me of John Belushi, and that's why I loved him; he was a big physical guy who had no problem throwing himself into something all the way, all the time. So in October 1997, I was surprised to enter a Thai restaurant called Toi on Sunset Boulevard late one night—about two a.m.—with a friend to have dinner, only to find Chris in the back of the place with his brother and several porn stars and strippers. He saw me and exploded: "Leif, Leif fucking Garrett! Hey, girls, do you know who this is? We're going to party all night tonight!" He was a fan from the old days—at least a fan of the excess I had come to represent, I guess. And so off we went. I wasn't into doing coke then, but Chris insisted and so we did. He was hard to keep up with. We went to party up in Coldwater Canyon; I watched him walk up the hill and didn't think he was going to make it. He was wheezing and heaving. "You gonna be okay?" I asked him. He didn't look like he was going to make it.

We got home at dawn, and I think his brother was pretty upset. They were headed back to New York City that morning, as Chris was returning to host *Saturday Night Live*. He died the following December, at just thirty-three years old, from cocaine and morphine. I was heartbroken. It reminded me of when John Belushi had died. And it made me wonder how much longer I was going to be around too.

I was tired of watching people die—people I knew, people who were talented. I had also been good friends with Sam Kinison, who was killed in a car crash several years earlier, in 1992. Like Chris and John, he was another rambunctious individual who left a huge mark on the planet. I remember talking to him one night, and he told me he was so tired of lying about his true dreams and desires, and that's why he got into comedy. He said, "Life is too short to not do something you really believe in. So I turned in the collar for the cap. I turned in the cross for the coke." That was him; that's what he wanted to do. Even though I was a heroin addict, there were still things I wanted to do.

1997: Chris Farley

Lots of things. I still wanted to get back into acting, and I absolutely wanted to sing. I didn't want to be a casualty. But I didn't know what to do about it. I had nobody to help. I was lonely, and I missed my former life, even the fake parts—it was better than where I was now.

1998: The Death of David MacLeod

In December 1998 I got a phone call from Michelle Phillips. "Leif," she said, "did you hear about David MacLeod? He was found dead." I had not heard the news. I had lost track of him over the years.

An Associated Press wire story explained what had happened. Thursday, December 31, 1998:

> A former Hollywood producer and convicted pedophile found dead on a downtown Montreal street died of an irregular heartbeat, a coroner said Thursday. But what exactly caused David Leigh MacLeod's heart to stop will not be known until toxicology tests are completed, said Dr. Paul Dionne of the Quebec coroner's office.
>
> MacLeod, a first cousin of actors Warren Beatty and Shirley MacLaine, was found dead Dec. 6 near an overpass. He was 54....
>
> MacLeod had a lengthy criminal record and was wanted in the United States by the FBI and New York City police in the investigation of several prostitution cases involving teenage boys. MacLeod had been a fugitive since Dec. 14, 1989, when he

bolted from a New York courthouse where he faced 15 charges of endangering the welfare of children and criminal solicitation. His criminal record went back as far as 1974, when he was convicted in a child molestation case in Toronto. He got a suspended sentence.

It's the last sentence that got me. He was already a convicted child molester when he first approached my mother and got to know me in the mid-1970s. He didn't have to troll young victims. He could just arrange a casting session.

By the way, later there was some talk about how he really died. To some, it appeared more suspicious than originally reported. To some, it appeared that it may have been an act of retribution by a parent of one of the victims.

What more has to happen? How many more young people need to be lured into potentially catastrophic situations that will scar them for the rest of their lives? As I sit here telling my story, I'm horrified at certain scenarios I was forced to experience, scenarios I survived, and I think about kids this could be happening to at this very second, with nobody stepping in to help them, defend them, or protect them. How many more "grooming" stories do we need to hear? And it's not being done just by celebrities. Grooming has become a sophisticated tactic when it comes to how adults in general prey on youth. From the time I was sixteen, I made a conscious decision to not bring children into this world because, I'm sorry, I think it's too crazy and dangerous a place. It scares me to think of raising children today.

Behind the Music

In late 1998, I needed money for heroin, plain and simple. I had never heard of the documentary series *Behind the Music* on the cable channel VH1, so when the producers contacted me, I didn't care what kind of show they were talking about. I cared only about the fact that they would pay me money. I wasn't watching TV. I didn't have cable. I didn't know what anything was. All I knew was they were going to sit me down in a hotel for two weekends in a row in Los Angeles and pay me a substantial amount of money for my time being interviewed. That was it. They were also going to be talking to several other people from my past, including my mother, my cousin, Peter, Michael Lloyd, and my manager, Stan. I didn't think much of it. I wanted money to buy drugs. That was it.

If you ever watch the show, you'll notice that there are two distinctly different interview personalities that I have on it. One of them is bright-eyed and clearheaded, and actually I seem pretty normal. In some segments though (in which I am wearing the black bandanna), I look high because I am high. I was sitting there on camera talking about how I had stopped taking drugs, and I was skulking off to the bathroom and smoking heroin, thinking stupidly that nobody would even smell it. It's how clueless addicts are. You live in such a rancid little bubble that you think nobody notices anything. That said, nobody said anything to me, so I thought I was getting away with it. I watch it today and it makes me sick. I was sitting there lying. (I wish I knew why people are so obsessed with me and drugs. I have always, even as a shy child, been rebellious—the more someone says "don't" I almost automatically "do." I guess I just want to know about everything, firsthand, within reason).

A lot of the questions on camera were fairly innocuous. I was talking about my life and some things I had gone through. We touched upon a few things, but nothing went very deep. There was very little discussion about my management and how I had been made to sing certain things I didn't want to sing. I'd heard they didn't want to press that too hard for fear of being sued by the Scotti brothers. But what pissed me off was what they did to me in regard to Roland Winkler. I had not seen Roland since visiting him in the hospital the day after that tragic accident back in November 1979. It's not that I didn't want to see him, but once the lawyers got involved, I wasn't allowed to see him. I promised him in that hospital room that I would do everything I could to pay for his situation the rest of my life. And I meant it. But once the lawyers got involved, what I said made no difference. I wasn't allowed near him. And then after all of the settlements in the mid-1980s, I never saw him again. There was nothing that brought us together. Look, we hadn't been good friends in the first place, but obviously we were joined forever by that terrible and fateful night. I talked about the car crash on the *Behind the Music* episode. I described what that night was like, in minimal detail. Then at one point they told me they had located Roland. Huh? I had no idea where he lived or what his life was like at that point. I just knew he had been paralyzed. The news caught me so off guard that, as you can see on the show, I broke down crying and walked off camera. It hit me like a ton of bricks that they knew where he was. I had blocked that whole night out of my life for so long that when it all came back during these interviews, I got very emotional. It was such a scary and horrific moment that night. What happened to that poor guy was terrible. But what the producers did next is something that still bothers me after all of these years. They had me driving around in the producer's car, an old-school repainted checker cab like you see in New York City. It appeared as if I was driving my own car, and they told me they needed some driving shots of me. So we were cruising around the San Fernando Valley, and they were giving me directions to go someplace. Then, at the last minute, they sprung on me that we were actually going to see Roland. I said, "Are you kidding me? I don't know if I'm up for that. I'm not prepared." The producers and the cameraman were stressing to me, "This will be really good for the show. Trust us, this is good television. It's going to be okay. He wants to see you."

Well, by that point we were pretty much at the park, and I could see the other camera crew set up. There was no way of getting out of this. So I went along with it. Just as I had always done in my career, I did what I was told. I was obedient, and I played along. Old habits die hard. Obviously when we did see each other, it was a very emotional moment. When he told me that what happened that night had actually saved his life because of the path he was on, it blew my mind. It still does. It broke my heart seeing the condition he was in, but it filled my heart to know that somebody could be that selfless. (During the writing of this book, Roland passed away, and when I heard the news I sat in my bedroom and wept. It brought everything back.) I wasn't prepared for the meeting that afternoon, and I didn't want to do it. But it was a compelling reunion—there's no denying that; again, if you see the show, you'll see it's emotional and real. And that was it. I took the money and ran. I bought more drugs.

Dave Navarro was a fan of the series and told me that when my episode aired, he was going to have a little party at his house up in the Hollywood Hills. I was hanging out up there a lot at that point; I thought it sounded like fun. Of course, the joke was going to be that I was going to be sitting there on television talking about how I no longer did heroin while I (along with everyone else) would be sitting in the house doing heroin while watching.

It was all so screwed up. Dave was a totally cool guy, but he had his own drug issues, obviously, as did everybody else there that night. I was walking in and out of the room the whole time the show was on; I actually had a hard time watching. Even in the bad shape I was in then, I hated watching myself lying. I have always prided myself on being basically an honest person. For better or worse, I was honest. But there I was lying through my teeth. It hurt and made me sad to see myself doing that. But what I never expected was the attention the show generated. It must've struck a chord because literally over-night my publicist started getting hundreds and hundreds of letters expressing love and support for me. People hadn't seen me for so long—a lot of people even thought I was dead—and the show in this sense resurrected me and all of the feelings people had about me back in the late 1970s. And when they saw how far I had fallen, it made them want to reach out to me. I hadn't seen this coming. I had done the show only for the money. But that show became one of the most talked-about things on television. It was like everybody had seen it. I heard it got the highest ratings VH1 had ever had. It caught me off guard, and when I read the letters from people, I have to admit I was touched.

> Leif, I have been very upset by what has happened to you. I am a 40-year-old woman who grew up with posters on my wall of you. I had all of your albums and idolized you. I am praying for you and your recovery over your addiction.

> Leif and I knew each other years ago when I was editor of *16* and several other teen magazines. Leif's intelligence, wisdom and humor was well beyond his years; he was a standout as a person-ality, and I enjoyed every visit and phone call. Please tell Leif my prayers are with him today, as they have been all these years.

> Just a brief note to let you know that many people here in Australia are thinking of you and that you are in our prayers. I grew up being a fan of yours in the 70's [sic] and I hope that

this year will bring you much healing, restoration, and renewed energy to enjoy sharing your music again with the world.

As *LA Weekly* wrote at the time:

For one brief moment, Leif Garrett was the Backstreet Boys, 'N Sync and 98 Degrees all rolled into one pretty little toy boy with a blond shag and skintight pants. An adorably androgynous gold mine, he was the quintessential teen idol. But by 1980, his bubble-gum bubble had burst, and he disappeared. That is, until January 1999, when VH1 first aired his life story in a phenomenally popular Behind the Music. It was a tale that had it all—the show became a ratings juggernaut, airing in heavy rotation for over a year. It also set off a whole new wave of Leifmania. Old fans re-emerged, as devoted as ever. New fans found themselves inexplicably drawn to this sexy yet troubled man.

As *LA Weekly* said, a 2.0 version of "Leifmania" was born as a result of that TV show, and I decided to try to capitalize on it. I mean, I had very little else going on in my life. I still needed money for drugs, but I also decided that I wanted to get back into making music. You have to remember, I never wanted to stop making music. Even when I was faking it as a teen idol, I always wanted to be better. I always wanted to be a strong singer. I always wanted to write music. Maybe this was an opportunity for me to try to salvage my life and be what I wanted to be on my terms. I had no idea if it was possible, but I decided to give it a shot. I put together a music band/project called "Godspeed" and released an EP that featured, in addition to my band, my old friend Dave Navarro (playing piano); Marilyn Manson guitarist Zim Zum also contributed. Rosie O'Donnell had me and the band on her show, which was cool. Evidently she had been moved by the VH1 documentary, and that's why she had me on. After that I went out on the road with the band I loved, the Melvins, joining them onstage every night to perform a cover of the Nirvana classic "Smells Like Teen Spirit" (while also playing an opening set). Even though I was still struggling with my drug use, I loved these musical projects. I think a lot of it had to do with the fact that I was now completely in control of what I was singing and how I was singing. That's what felt so good. I expanded my musical experiences a couple of years later by creating a new band, F8. We got in a motor home and toured the United States several times across, old-school style, driving together like a band—like I would've loved to back in the days when I was a teen idol. We played a mix of classic rock covers and original songs. I know that some people came out just to see me because I was a curiosity. But I also know that many of those people stayed after the show to tell me how much they enjoyed it. They had not expected that from me. Making a living as a musician is very hard to do in this day and age. But after being on the road with a real band, I knew that making music was something I would be doing in some capacity the rest of my life. Touring in the early to mid-2000s finally made me believe that maybe I wasn't such a fraud after all when it came to getting behind a microphone and fronting a band.

What You Do for Money

Did anybody see the movie *Party Line*? Or *Cheerleader Camp*? How about *Delta Fever*? It's amazing what people do when they need money for drugs. I admit it, I did what I had to do to make money. I still went out on auditions, and look, beggars can't be choosers. Am I proud of those movies? No. But I was doing what I had to do to survive. Even if it meant surviving as a junkie. When I was hired for something, I showed up, I was professional, and I got the job done. That was something that hadn't changed from when I was child on set. Throughout the 2000s, I did other things, including some stage work, like playing the title role in *Joseph and the Amazing Technicolor Dream Coat*. In 2000, I also appeared in the National Theatre of the Deaf's production of *A Child's Christmas in Wales*. One of my favorite theatrical experiences was appearing in summer stock at The Barn Theatre's production of *Old Timer* in 2001. That year I also voiced an episode of *Family Guy*, re-creating my talk with Roland when we were reunited on the *Behind the Music* special (the producers didn't want to pay for the rights to license the original audio). I was doing what I had to do to make a living, and making a living, as I've said, around this time had a lot to do with buying drugs. But it doesn't mean that some of the work wasn't interesting and satisfying. Did I think it was a good thing to appear on the short-lived CMT show *Ty Murray's Celebrity Bull Riding Challenge*? No. And thank god I never actually got around to getting on a live bull. There was a dating show I did that I found embarrassing as well. But again, money. I did actually enjoy winning the celebrity edition of *Fear Factor* in 2006. That netted me fifty thousand dollars, and believe it or not, I was using drugs during the production of the show. In 2008, I joined the cast of what was then titled *The Smoking Gun Presents: World's Dumbest* on truTV. That fit me well, simply adding comedic commentary to footage of criminals. And there were some movies that I enjoyed. In 2005, I appeared with Aaron Carter in *Popstar*. Before that, a couple of years earlier, I appeared as myself in the David Spade film *Dickie Roberts: Former Child Star*. I even cowrote and sang the title song for the film's soundtrack. More and more, it seemed that music was the art form that ultimately I would spend the rest of my life doing.

Arrests

This is an overview of some of my arrest history for narcotics. I was arrested for possession of cocaine in 2004. I pleaded guilty in March 2005 to attempted possession of cocaine-based narcotics and was placed on probation. When I failed to appear in court in December 2005 for a status report, a warrant was issued for my arrest. On January 14, 2006, when I was arrested on a Los Angeles Metro Rail platform for not having a ticket, police found heroin on me. Because of the outstanding warrant for violating probation in a cocaine-related arrest, I was held without bail. I agreed to join a strict drug-diversion program, and my release from jail was ordered. I dropped out of the rehabilitation program and was taken into custody again on March 30 after a Superior Court commissioner determined that I had failed several drug tests while staying in a live-in drug-diversion program. At that point I acknowledged that I needed more help. On May 11, after failing to complete court-ordered drug rehabilitation, I was sentenced to ninety days in jail and three years' probation. I was given credit for the jail time I had already served since March 30.

On February 1, 2010, I was arrested again for possession of narcotics. After denying having any drugs in my possession, I finally admitted to police that I had black tar heroin in my shoe. I posted ten thousand dollars for bail and was charged with a felony count of heroin possession. On October 18, 2010, I pleaded no contest to heroin possession in Los Angeles and entered a court-ordered rehabilitation program.

I hate revisiting these portions of my life. They are the darkest and worst things I have ever been through. I've tried to block them from my memory, but it's hard. When you're addicted to drugs, you don't remember a lot about your days; they become one for so long. When I was addicted, I lost touch with pretty much everybody who meant anything to me, except for my mom. I have to say she was always there by my side for whatever I needed. For all of the differences we have had over the years as well as the questions I still have about my upbringing and the way things were done, my mom has always been there for me. She's not perfect, but none of us is.

The first time I got arrested in an LA subway station, I think it's because I looked like a junkie. I was that bad. Undercover cops have a good eye for guys like that, so it was pretty easy to peg me as a user. For one, I was wearing dark glasses at night. I was an easy mark. One of the cops said to me after they stopped me, "You work with us and we will let you go. Just tell us where the stuff is." I was a junkie. I stupidly trusted them. I took my shoe off and showed them where the heroin was, and they cuffed me. "But I thought you said...?" "I don't deal with junkies, asshole." And they dragged me out to the car.

The second time I got busted for heroin, it was in the exact same place. What are the odds of that? I passed through the turnstile to go get on a train. I had about three hundred bucks in my back pocket and black tar heroin in my shoe, just like last time. So the cop said to me, "Hey, man, that show you were on, *World's Dumbest Criminals*, is really hilarious!" I called out, "Thanks, man!" over my shoulder. Obviously I didn't want to hang out too long and have a conversation. "Gotta run!"

I heard another cop behind the first cop ask, "Who is that?" And the other guy answered, "He's the one that got popped last year, remember? The teen idol? That's the same guy." Great. Behind me I heard two sets of footsteps coming toward me and then felt the inevitable hand on the back of my shoulder. "Hey, kid, where do you think you're going?"

Then there was the mug shot. I know everybody talks about that thing. It kills me, seeing it today. I had stared into the lenses of so many renowned photographers. My picture had been taken tens, if not hundreds, of thousands of times over the years. I knew how to work the camera. Knowing how was a big part of my life, after all. I was as much a model as I was a singer. But then I had to look into that lens for my mug shot. That's how the world was going to get reacquainted with me. How shocked everybody must've been. But what can I tell you? That was me. As sad as it seems, that's what my life had become. Everybody freaked out because the hair was gone. Guess what? That happens sometimes. When people stop me on the street and say nasty things about that, I don't know what to tell them. It's called getting older, and it's okay. We have this cultural thing that no celebrities are ever supposed to grow old before our eyes.

Then it was into jail for ninety days. Gone was the rooftop suite at the Dorchester Hotel in London. Now it was a nine-by-six cell, one of twelve individual cells, and I was sandwiched between a pedophile priest and one of Suge Knight's henchmen. Awesome. What can I say about prison? It's the absolute worst. I wanted to be in protective custody, which meant I had to do the full ninety-day sentence. Had I agreed to be in the general population, I would have been out of there in four days. But I don't think I would've made it out. It wasn't worth it to me. I had heard too many stories about what might happen to me in that kind of environment, so I opted for the complete sentence.

The first day I was there, one of the female guards pushed an old photo of me from *Tiger Beat* into my cell. "Look at you now, you fucking loser," she said, chuckling. I didn't think that was right. I had been arrested; I had broken the law and accepted my sentence. But I didn't need that bullshit. I'm sorry, but I don't think it's right to humiliate people like that. But, of course, I had no say in the matter. I ignored her. My mom visited occasionally, and other times I would get an alert that there was somebody there. But they don't tell you who's waiting for you. You need to go up there and check it out and then decide if you want to have that visitor spend time with you. Several times there were fans who had come to visit me, but I had no interest in talking with anybody except my mom and a couple of very close friends. I was miserable.

My bail bondsman, Chris Cox, gave me occasional updates on my case, but there wasn't too much to report. Of course, being locked up meant I couldn't do drugs, and so that forced me to go cold turkey. I dealt with it okay. There had been times leading up to my incarceration when I did not use drugs for several months, so it wasn't that big a deal for me. Don't get me wrong, I was craving heroin. But I could deal with that.

For the most part, my entire world existed in semidarkness, with a dim fluorescent light overhead, a television that was blasting constantly, and food that was so horrible I can barely describe it. The first day that I was there, they brought a plate of noodles that had what appeared to be pencil erasers in it. I couldn't even guess what they were made out of, but I certainly wasn't going to eat them.

The next day they brought a bologna sandwich, and the meat was green. If you're in prison and you've got somebody on the outside who can get money to you, then you can use what's called the canteen, which basically has food from vending machines, like chips and Ramen noodles. That's what I opted for, obviously. But the only water I got for the Ramen noodles was lukewarm, so it did not do any good.

Given the amount of time I had on my hands, I spent most of it reading. I read some of the Anne Rice vampire books and got into the Harry Potter books. Those were good. The stories were nice and escapist, and I thought the characters were well-drawn. I also took a lot of time to think. What was I doing there? How had I gotten to that point in my life? Was it just about being a little boy in search of a father? Or was it more about having been a fraud for so many years that I didn't care what I did to myself? Was I simply trying to kill myself? Maybe it was all three. I'm still not sure.

Jail is a horrible place. You feel like an animal. You are treated like an animal. But in the absence of any real stimulation—mental, physical, or otherwise—a kind of clarity starts to reveal itself after a few days. I had never been alone like this. I mean, in my case in particular, I may have been the most overstimulated person of my generation. For a number of years, every single minute I was awake, something extreme was happening, for better or worse. I also had never been made to quit drugs cold turkey. I was sick and hungry. But again, this was an opportunity I could never remember having. Nothing but time.

In the void, I started to self-analyze a bit. I'm not sure if it was even deliberate, but it just started happening. All of a sudden, I could honestly judge things that had happened in my life. I thought back to the accident in 1979. I could have easily died. Roland and I both could have. What happened to Roland was tragic. But I'd never stopped to think about how close I came to death that night. What would it have been like had I died? How would I have been remembered? Would it be sort of like James Dean? Death in a fiery Porsche accident. Taken from the world while still beautiful and mysterious. No chance to erode before people's eyes. A wistful, what-could-have-been story that might have grown larger over the years. Maybe that would have been better. I mean, what I had become was a disgrace. It was a very hard thing to confront. In that jail cell, alone and lonely, I was forced to accept that part of me wished I had died that night. And then I came face-to-face with the bleak reality that I had been trying to kill myself ever since.

2010: Back to Korea

In 2010, I finally got a break after all the courtroom drama and jail time and arrests. It was an offer to go back to Korea and perform in celebration of the thirtieth anniversary of my first trip there. I was kind of nervous at first, but I knew I had to do it. If I wanted to get back into singing—if I wanted to prove myself—this would be the way to do it. There were a lot of people and a lot of attention. We headed over there and performed a series of shows. Women brought their children. It was amazing. There were thousands of people who knew all the words to all of the old songs. It took me back to the craziness of 1980, when I was the first American pop artist to play over there.

And it was exciting for me to be back onstage. I knew a lot of people had counted me out, but I wanted to show everybody that I still had some gas left in the tank. Up on the stage, singing "I Was Made for Dancing" actually felt good. I had grown up. It wasn't like the old days. I was there on my own terms. As I stood on that stage, my mind flashed back to what it had been like being in Korea the first time. Maybe there was hope for me. I looked out at the crowd, and everyone was going crazy. They believed me. It wasn't over. There was another road for me. And I was going to take it.

I was broken, I had challenges, but I also had hope. It's very hard to describe how healing it can be looking out into a crowd and feeling nothing but love bouncing back. My life up to that point had been an amazing roller coaster with thrilling highs and desperate lows. Could I have used a little bit more middle ground to round things out and keep me centered? Perhaps, but we don't always get to decide all of those things.

One thing I know is that I've taken the life that has been given to me and I haven't always valued it perhaps the way I should. But as I look down the road now, I know what I want to do. I know I want to keep making music; I know I want to act; I know I want to be responsible; I know I want to be a good person. Despite everything that's happened to me, I still don't think I would trade any of it because it has made me what I am. I'm a survivor, but I'm also a dreamer. I believe in the good of people. I'm positive. I will always believe that love is the most important, unifying force on the planet. For all of the love that I have felt from so many of you over the years, thank you so much. Now let's get on with the rest of the show.

Epilogue

This book has been a long time coming. I'd been asked many times before to do a memoir, but I knew that I wasn't ready. I believe that I had issues I needed to deal with, as well as some of my friends to deal with, and my respect for them is immense. I don't kiss and tell. Since the only way to write one's life is honestly, I also didn't want the memoir to come from a bitter or angry place. I have lived an incredible life thus far, and I want this path to remain available. Why burn bridges to sell books? I'm very fond of my memories, and I have so many more that I would love to share. But I believe that the adventures in this book are the ones I need to talk about first. I've always been one to believe that in order to understand something, you must experience it firsthand. This is my reality, and I believe the truth of it has molded and shaped me to a large degree into who I am. I believe the truth will set us free; I believe that honesty is the best policy; I believe in love, not war. I think that communication is paramount and it's better to listen than talk about something you don't know about. And don't be afraid to ask questions. Never stop learning because the minute you do, you stagnate and die. I want to thank everyone for enriching my life. We are all the children of a higher power, and together we can make things happen.

Postscript

I also want to make you, the reader, aware that my coauthor, Chris, and I did reach out to Tony Scotti to get his thoughts about the time he spent with me while I was under contract with his management company. These are the exact questions and answers as they were given via email. Several of the answers surprised me and, quite frankly, troubled me. I will let you be your own judge.

Q: **What first interested you in Leif as a client?**
A: Leif was brought to me by Michael Lloyd as a potential future teen idol. He wanted to see if our company had any interest in recording and managing Leif.

Q: **What were the goals you had for him as a recording artist?**
A: We believed that Leif could develop into a mainstream pop/ rock singer.

Q: **What were the biggest challenges in developing Leif's' recording career?**
A: All teen idols have difficulty crossing from a teen image to that of a serious rocker. That's the reason why we put Leif on Atlantic

Records. Atlantic never had a teen artist like Leif and Atlantic Records had rock credibility. We believed that this would enhance his credibility with radio, and it did.

Q: Was the process with Leif collaborative; was he allowed to influence/affect/choose the kind of material he was recording?

A: No, the process was not collaborative. Leif would express his opinion but we did what we thought was necessary for him to have a successful career.

Q: What do you view as your company's biggest success with Leif?

A: Leif had many successes, but the fact that we successfully launched him all over the world at that time was unique for a teen artist and gave him stature.

Q: What do you view as your company's biggest failure with Leif?

A: I never wanted Leif and his musicians to play live on TV. Television mixing in those days was never complimentary to the artist. Our experience was that most rock artists would refuse to sing live and preferred not to be on TV if they had to, unless they were in control of the mixing. When Leif was doing promotion in foreign countries he made the decisions whether or not to sing live. These performances did not always advance his popularity.

Q: How important was Leif to the development of your record label/management company?

A: Leif never sold enough records to materially contribute to our company, but we loved him and always had high hopes for his future.

Q: Do you have any regrets over how your company handled Leif's career?

A: No regrets. We did our best.

Postscript

Q: **What is your personal fondest memory from working with Leif?**

A: Leif was a handsome and charming young boy. I always enjoyed meeting with him.

Q: **What is your personal most difficult memory from working with Leif?**

A: Leif was young. Everyone he met had an opinion about his music; his career; his family and his future. This makes life difficult for a young boy trying to find himself. I don't believe he had a father figure in life and was often confused about whom to trust. Leif had the same problem that many young boys have growing up, but his was more difficult because he was growing up in the public eye.

Afterword
by Chris Epting

"Dude, look at my arm." We were in Leif's kitchen, and he was making us breakfast on the first day we got together to talk about the possibility of working on his book together. We got started right away talking about music we loved growing up, and we automatically both zeroed in on *Goodbye Yellow Brick Road* as a game-changer album. We both started talking about how much we loved the artwork on the inside gatefold, and that's when he stopped me and held his arm out. He had goose bumps. "Dude, look at my arm." The hair on his arms was standing on end. "I think maybe we're going to be able to work together, man," he said. I felt the same way.

I always knew that Leif had many amazing stories to tell. I just wasn't sure if he was ever going to be in the mood to do it. I had reached out to him a couple of years earlier but heard back from his representative that he wasn't interested in writing his memoirs. Not yet, anyhow. Then, out of the blue, I received a note back a couple of years later asking if I still might be interested in at least opening up a conversation. I absolutely was. Leif and I are pretty much the exact same age. When he was busy becoming a teen idol, I was into the Sex Pistols, the Stones, Zeppelin, and lots of other bands like that. So was he. You just never would've known it by the kind of press coverage he got back in the late 1970s.

I didn't read teen magazines. It wasn't until I caught part of his special on CBS in the spring of 1979 that I got a true sense of what Leif Garrett was all about. I was at a high school party and stumbled into a room with a girl. The TV was on, and we both watched part of the show. He was interesting. There was a lot more going on there than I would've imagined. He was funny. He seemed smart too. I'd always thought he was a good child actor. I saw him on so many different things and always found him versatile. But on the variety show there was something different about him. That stuck with me. As the decades rolled on, I would always pay attention when his name popped up in the headlines. Unfortunately, the headlines were usually not very positive. It could've been a car accident or a motorcycle accident.

And then came the time when the VH1 *Behind the Music* episode aired in 1999.

I found it riveting. I found it sad. But I also found it very compelling. Here was a complicated man at odds with many things, but also interested in trying to make a better life for himself.

That morning in his kitchen, I had no idea about the friendship that was about to begin taking hold. That's been the best part of this entire experience for me: I've made this amazing new friend. I think we've written a wonderful book together, and that's great. But friendships will always outlive books, and for that I'm truly thankful. When you write with somebody, you get to hear a lot. Or at least you should. If the process is going to work, it has to be very open and honest. You hear plenty of things that will never make it into the book, but you need to go through those walls to get to the other side. I've learned that on numerous occasions working with other people. But never have I worked with anybody who has this much to talk about. It's almost incomprehensible what Leif has experienced in his life. More highs and lows than you can even define. But one thing I always notice is that at the heart of it all is somebody I can relate to. Just another former American teenager who always appreciated sports, pretty girls, rock 'n' roll, cars, great books, great movies... He just happened to be somebody who got made into a teen idol. He's an incredibly sensitive person and one of the most generous people I have ever been around.

I think the truest form of Leif I have yet to witness was when we were walking down Sunset Boulevard one night. We were early for a concert and decided to grab a quick bite at a sushi bar. On the walk over from the Palladium, we passed many homeless people. I think Leif stopped for every single one to offer a couple of bucks or a few words of encouragement. After we ate and were headed back to the show on the other side of the street, he did the exact same thing. It didn't matter if we were running a little bit late. He took his time to help out his brothers on the street. But there was one guy out there that night who stood out to me: a young African American guy, maybe in his mid-twenties, who was not homeless but rather out there handing out his new music CDs. He had a good rap and was a good salesman for himself. When he stopped us and held a CD out, Leif took out ten bucks, gave it to him, and thanked him for the CD. Before letting us go, the guy said to us, "You better listen to that, man. You are going to love it; it's really great." Leif said, "I can't wait. I promise I will." And the guy said, "Really, many people are going to love this. The girls are really going to love this. All the young girls are going to have my picture up on their bedroom walls; you'll see. They will listen and then sit there and stare at pictures of me." He should only have known whom he was speaking to. Leif got a small grin on his face and said to the guy, "Listen, man, here's my advice; you can take it if you want. Just focus on the music. That's what it's all about. I know it seems cool to want your picture up on someone's wall. But trust me, focus on the music and really good things can happen. That's way more important than the pictures." The guy smiled and said, "Thank you, man. You sound like a man who knows what he's talking about." And we moved on. Again, he should have only known.

I sincerely hope you enjoyed this book. I'm proud of my friend for telling his story. And I'm deeply grateful he trusted me to help him in the process.

* * *

As always, I want to thank my family first. Writing books can be a very consuming process, and it truly requires love, understanding, and especially patience of those closest to you. In that respect, I'm deeply grateful for my wife, Jean; our son, Charlie; and our daughter, Claire. There were also many people who helped with the creation of this book, terrific resources who were generous with their time, images, etc. In particular, I would like to thank Michael Lloyd, Peter Underwood, Brad Elterman, and Tony Scotti for answering our questions. I would also like to thank Marcy Massura, Barbara Papageorge, and especially Leif's mom, Carolyn Stellar, not just for her good company but also for her precious memories and vivid details. She has written a book herself that I have had the pleasure of assisting her with, and hopefully one day soon you'll get a chance to enjoy it. Thank you to our literary agent, John Silbersack, and everyone at Post Hill Press, including Anthony Ziccardi, Maddie Sturgeon, Devon Brown, and Heather Steadham. Writing and releasing a book are team efforts, and we certainly have a good team behind *Idol Truth*. Last but not least, thank you to Leif Garrett. Dude, I am so proud of you. I appreciate your trusting me with your story, but more than that, I'm most grateful for the friendship that has grown from this project. I love you, brother, will always be here for you, and I look forward to what the future holds. You are the real deal. Please don't ever forget that.